gok
MY AUTOBIOGRAPHY
wan

Through Thick and Thin

EBURY
PRESS

5 7 9 10 8 6

This edition published 2011
First published in 2010 by Ebury Press, an imprint of Ebury Publishing
A Random House Group company

The Random House Group Limited Reg. No. 954009

Addresses for companies within the Random House Group can be found
at www.randomhouse.co.uk

A CIP catalogue record for this book is available from the British Library

The Random House Group Limited supports The Forest Stewardship
Council (FSC®), the leading international forest certification organisation.
Our books carrying the FSC label are printed on FSC® certified paper. FSC
is the only forest certification scheme endorsed by the leading
environmental organisations, including Greenpeace. Our paper
procurement policy can be found at www.randomhouse.co.uk/environment

B
WAN

Designed and set by seagulls.net

Printed and bound by CPI Group (UK) Ltd, Croydon, CRO 4YY

ISBN 9780091938383

To buy books by your favourite authors and register for offers visit
www.randomhouse.co.uk

To Maya and Lola. I love you more than the world and a moment longer than the rest of time. I hope that one day you will read this book and learn from my mistakes. I promise, you will never be alone ... not for as long as I live.

Uncle Gok x

Note from the author

This book is based entirely on my memories. No memory is infallible and I'm sure some people will remember things differently, but this is my life through my eyes – the way I recall it. Sit back, take a load off and I hope you enjoy the ride.

Contents

Through Thick
and Thin

Grandma's Eggs

INGREDIENTS

2 large eggs
Salt
Light soya sauce

METHOD

Boil eggs for around 10 minutes, or until hard. Rinse under cold water and crack and peel off the shells. Place in a small bowl and coarsely chop with a dinner knife. Add a pinch of salt and 4–6 dashes of light soya sauce. Eat with a dessertspoon and think about your family and how very special they are to you.

PROLOGUE

Food

I have always loved food. It would have been hard not to, when food has always been at the centre of my world. I joke with my mum that I came out of her with a pair of chopsticks in my hand and if she'd greeted me with a loving maternal smile instead of handing me a bowl of noodles, then I might have liked sports and not spring rolls!

Food is everything to my family. We not only needed food to live, like everyone else; we also needed food to survive financially. It was our livelihood. All my life, my parents have run restaurants of one kind or another so the family was always surrounded by food and we all heartily enjoyed it. The family motto was: If it makes you feel good, eat it. We fed customers constantly but we made sure that we stayed loyal to our own mealtimes and the custom of eating together. We still do.

Within five minutes of us getting together, we always start either discussing food or eating it. A visit home to Leicester would not be complete without dim sum at my auntie's restaurant or a home-cooked meal that my mum and brother will have carefully prepared. When we eat out as a family, we still fall into our familiar roles. Dad will sit at the head of the table with Mum next to him. I will sit with my sister and my brother's children, and my brother and his wife will join us to finish the set. Dad always orders the meal. The waitress arrives with pots of boiling oolong tea and as she pours it out, Dad'll ask us what we fancy. The answer is always the same: 'Whatever, Dad. You decide.'

With that, he will rattle off in Chinese an extensive list of dishes. Because none of us, except my father, speaks Chinese, the meal can sometimes contain some surprises. We never know what has been ordered but, more often than not, we can guess the usual suspects. As the dishes begin to arrive, we congratulate my father on his ordering: 'Mmm, stuffed peppers and black bean ... delicious' or 'I've not had juk in ages, has it got pork in it?' or 'Stewed bean-curd hot pot ... mmm ... Not as good as yours, though, Dad!' Then we work our way through each dish, marvelling at how fresh the fish is or rejoicing at how crispy the noodles are. All Chinese restaurants serve the food at the centre of the table so we share our favourite morsels with one another. Mum loves Chinese mushrooms, so you can guarantee that as soon as she has finished one, another is passed by one of us. Lisa, my sister-in-law, likes the white rice wrapping around the hau gau but not the prawn filling. My brother will carefully dissect a dumpling, expertly disembowel the filling and eating it, before passing the white wrapping over to her – chopstick martial arts!

There is always a big bowl of boiled rice. By tradition, the youngest able person at the table inherits the responsibility of serving the rice. When I was the youngest child in the family, this tradition of thousands of years was passed to me. I remember the joy of doing my part, and I loved the feeling of importance when I fulfilled the honoured role. I still have moments, when serving the rice, of absolute happiness because to me, rice symbolises stability, unity and togetherness. Food means love and family.

But somewhere along the line, food came to mean too much to me. It became my best friend; it brought me happiness, warmth, security and comfort. It became my addiction, my secret, my everything. My days were spent thinking about and acquiring food because only then could I be happy. I was a compulsive overeater, partly because I ate the wrong things (I was surrounded by westernised restaurant food all the time) and at the wrong times (it was quite normal to sit down to a big meal in the middle of the night in my family, when my parents got back from the restaurant), and partly because I grew to love it too much. The effect of food on my body was appalling as I ballooned outwards, beginning as a chubby child and ending up as a morbidly obese young adult who felt confused, unworthy and rejected.

Food had done this to me, but in doing so, it had become my only escape from a world that looked at me and laughed, taunted, bullied and threatened. Food then became my enemy. Food and I had to do battle ... and it was a struggle that almost killed me. I think that, in the end, food holds the secret to my entire life.

CHAPTER ONE

Where It All Began

I don't know how I got fat. Well, of course I know how I got fat – eating like a grown soldier at the age of three was how I got fat – but what I mean is, I don't remember going from a thin boy to a fat boy with boobs. There are very few pictures of me as child (so few that for many years my sister teased me that I was adopted) and, as a result, I don't know exactly when it happened.

The last evidence of me being slim is a photograph taken before I started school, so I'm about four years old. In it, I am standing outside my granddad's restaurant, The Hung Lau – Leicester's first Chinese restaurant. He opened it in the late sixties, and it's where my dad began his apprenticeship. I'm posing for the camera, wearing Dad's Aviator sunglasses, shorts and a *Jungle Book* t-shirt (even then I was never shy of a camera, and my campness was coming along nicely). By then, both my brother and sister were chubby, so I obviously didn't want to feel left out.

My sister Oilen is the oldest of us, four years my senior. She's sensible and very clever – Mum still tells how she wrote an entire book at the age of seven and I'm still impressed – and I've always looked up to her. Then there's Kwok-Lyn, my cheeky brother. He's only fifteen months older than me so when we were growing up, we were more like twins: Mum would dress us in identical clothes, our mannerisms were very similar and we giggled at the same things. I arrived on the scene last of all, born in 1974 and christened Kowkhyn, Gok for short. I was a very small baby – the family legend is that I was the weight of a bag of sugar when I was born and that when I came home, I was smaller than my first teddy bear. Even the tiniest nappy wouldn't fit me, so Mum used facecloths instead. The family called me 'Babe' and even though I was as robust as any of them, before long the nickname stuck.

The three of us siblings were similar and yet so different: Oilen was confident and academically gifted; Kwok-Lyn was strong and determined, but gentle. I was neither clever nor strong, but I made people laugh by being the joker and clowning around. I seemed to have a natural affinity with everyone, and I was always very tactile. I loved to hug people and always bonded well with them, particularly my female relatives, rushing up to them for cuddles when they came to visit. I used to tell my Auntie Dawn how beautiful she was, and I meant it. I could always see the beauty in women, even when very young.

Despite our differences, all three of us Wan children were hard workers, a virtue taught by our father, John Tung Shing Wan. He was born in a northern Hong Kong village – the kind where his mother caught fish for lunch in the morning – and emigrated to Britain with his family, arriving in Leicester in the sixties, where my grandfather then opened the Chinese restaurant where my father learned his trade.

While he was working there, my father took a trip to Southampton, where he met my mother, Myra, the innocent daughter of a cleaning lady single mother. They fell in love at once. My mum says that she knew from the day they met that he was the one, but the relationship was not an easy one for them. In the sixties, inter-racial marriages were virtually non-existent and they encountered a lot of prejudice and ostracism because of it. But they loved each other, stayed together and they've devoted their entire lives to the family they created. Their love for one another is so great, I sometimes think there could not have been any love in the world until they met. I regard my mum as the most successful woman in the world, as she has achieved what she wanted most: she found a man she loves and had a family which she will honour and care for until the day she dies.

Along with their other challenges, my parents had no money, surviving on my father's tiny wage from his family restaurant. When I was born, we were living in a static caravan in a park – I am the original trailer-park trash – then, as things got better, we moved to Beaumont Leys, the newest, poshest council estate in Leicester, made up of tiny terraces of smart, red-brick houses with white window frames and neatly picket-fenced back gardens. It was as though we'd arrived in our very own Oz (except that our yellow brick road was paved with prawn crackers). We were very happy in our house there, and my earliest memories are of being outside, playing in the garden in the summer sunshine with Mum. I had an affectionate and secure early child-hood, adoring my brother and sister and cosseted by the love of my parents.

When Kwok-Lyn started school, I missed him because up until then he had been my constant playmate, but it did feel good to be the centre of attention at home when the older ones were both at school. Every morning my mother would push me in the pushchair, while my brother and sister walked alongside, as we strolled through the estate where we lived and up the big hill to the school gates. When we got there, Mum would say, 'Wave goodbye and say "see you later".' I realise now that was her way of letting me know they were not leaving me for good, they were just growing up. Oilen was always keen to get into school – she was bright and eager to learn – while my brother would smile, gorgeous and cheeky, and run into class to join his friends.

No sooner had we left the gates of the school, I would turn in my pushchair and say, 'Mum, can we go and buy some sweets now? I promise I won't tell Kwok-Lyn and Oilen.' Most days Mum gave in to my request for sugary happiness, because she loved to spoil me a little. I usually chose a pick 'n' mix variety, as that made me feel I was getting more for my money; from an early age food was about quantity not quality. I would buy twenty half-penny gummy bears for a whole ten pence – beat that, Asda, with your bottom-spanking promises! – and I can still taste the acidic fruity flavours and the sticky jelly that got stuck in my teeth. Who knew then I was a gummy junkie?

Nowadays, if you ever lose me on the *How To Look Good Naked* set, you can almost always find me curled up in a corner, gossiping on my iPhone while demolishing an entire packet of Haribo Starmix! I adored my sweet treats, and my loving mother wanted to see me happy, so I soon came to expect as many goodies as I liked – and I liked a lot. I'd already begun my training in how (not) to eat.

When I was one year old, Dad moved away from the ties of his father's restaurant and opened his own business, The Bamboo House. It was the mid-seventies and the Bamboo was one of only a handful of Chinese restaurants in Leicester. It was in a fabulous location in the heart of the city centre, and everyone who was anyone in Leicester knew of my dad and the Bamboo, with its warm welcome and excellent food. The Bamboo came at just the right time: ready for the economic boom of the eighties, and my father would enjoy the resulting spending spree.

The Bamboo House attracted a mixed clientele, from businessmen to footballers and all those in between. The restaurant also became the location of choice for visiting actors from the Haymarket Theatre, and Dad can recall drunken evenings with the likes of Rod Hull and Jim Davidson at the restaurant (family legend has it that my father acted as therapist and confidant to Jim during one of his failing marriages).

Dad ran the business successfully for ten years and I spent a lot of time in the Bamboo. In fact, I have clearer memories of the restaurant than I do of our house in Beaumont Leys. Often, when we were really small, Dad would take my brother and me to work with him in the evening. We would dress up in mini tuxes and bow ties and my father would parade us proudly round the restaurant like little show ponies, well groomed and bright-eyed, while we enjoyed the attention. The women in the restaurant always made a huge fuss of me, telling me I was cute and letting me climb on their knees and hug them, which I loved.

Once I'd started school, my summer holidays were spent in the basement of the restaurant singing Abba songs with my sister, brother and Louise, a family friend's daughter. We would pretend to be the pop group sensation and I still hold a grudge for being forced to be Björn, the most uncharismatic of the group. We would dance round the basement, which was used as a storeroom for extra tables and chairs, and Oilen would choreograph us like we were a fully fledged tribute band. Using old Coke bottles as makeshift microphones, we mouthed the words of the songs and imitated the much-loved routines until we could perform them with precision and flare.

Upstairs in the restaurant, I would watch Dad greet his customers and welcome them in. He was a superb host – he knew his customers' favourite dishes, laughed at their jokes and asked them about their lives, remembering tiny details about their families, their health and their businesses. In return, his customers loved him and came back time and again to enjoy his welcome, the delicious food and the easy ambience. I so wanted to be my dad. He was so easy in his own skin, and as likeable and unchanging as a favourite meal. He was my hero, and still is.

By 1979, The Bamboo House was really thriving and the family was enjoying the financial benefits. Dad drove round in an oversized Jaguar and my mum had an extensive wardrobe of glamorous clothes that she wore to work each evening. We still lived in our council house on the estate, but the place was changing. Where once it had been as neat and pretty as Toytown, it was in fact still growing, sprawling outwards from the Beaumont

Leys shopping centre at its heart. As it grew, it was turning into one of the toughest places in Leicester, with lots of social problems, unemployment (despite the industrial estates nearby) and crime. I was too young, however, to see the growing poverty and hopelessness. It seemed to me that we lived without a care in our own cosy bubble, with its endless aroma of deep-fried love.

With things going so well, it wasn't long before Dad wanted to expand the business and he had decided to turn the Abba tribute band's rehearsal space into another dining room (bastard). Although business was good, my father had realised it would take more cash than he had to do the work so he had gone into partnership with a friend. Unfortunately, this idea did not go according to plan and soon after my dad had to sell his half of the restaurant to his partner. That was the end of The Bamboo House for us.

2 a.m. Steak

INGREDIENTS

One good slab of T-bone steak
Spanish onions
Button mushrooms
White long-grain rice
Vegetable oil
Remy Martin brandy
Salt and white pepper

METHOD

Wash the rice three times through cold water until the starch has been rinsed away, then place in a rice cooker and set to cook (approx. 20 minutes). Add 4 tablespoons of oil to a very hot wok and swill round until the entire surface is coated. When the oil begins to spit, add the chopped onions and mushrooms and a pinch of salt and pepper. Fry until golden. Once cooked, place the onions and mushrooms in a dish and cover to keep warm.

Add a further 4 tablespoons of oil to the wok and heat. Put in the steak and cook on one side for 3 minutes and the other for 2, adding salt and pepper to taste. When the steak is nearly cooked, carefully add a splash of brandy to the wok and swill quickly, with a beaming smile of success.

Spoon a generous helping of fluffy white rice on to a large 1980s dinner plate, and add the cooked onions and mushrooms to the side. Put the steak on the plate and pour the brandy oil over the rice and steak. Serve with a smearing of English mustard and eat at 2 a.m. when Mum and Dad have returned home from the restaurant.

Fabulous!

CHAPTER TWO

The Panda

After the disappointment of losing The Bamboo House, Dad decided he was going to start again, and he began looking at premises for a new restaurant. In 1984, he found an old three-storey building on the outskirts of Leicester city centre, on Fosse Road North. Although it had originally been an office building, Dad realised there was enough space to give us a home above and a business below, and his ambitious mind saw it as an investment. The restaurant was to be named The Panda. Dad's superstitious family warned him that the name was unlucky: because the panda is in danger of extinction, the restaurant would surely close in a matter of weeks. Dad was adamant. The Panda was the right name, so The Panda it was.

I was eleven when we left the estate and moved in to Fosse Road. I was hugely excited about living above the restaurant – it felt glamorous and modern and it would also mean we would see more of Mum and Dad. As with all businesses, especially catering, success does not come without a good ladle of hard work and, owing to the antisocial hours, Mum and Dad were not at home very much. It was hard for my parents to run a successful restaurant as well as raise three small children. Not a day passed when we wouldn't see them but our time together was never for very long. Mum would always take us to school in the morning and would always be at home when we returned at 3.30 p.m., while Dad was around as much as he could be, juggling his home life with the demands of running his business.

Sundays were our special day. The restaurant was closed for the only time in the week and we would always do something as a family – something fun, like going swimming or on a trip or out to the cinema. Food would always be a major part of the day. We'd start with a big breakfast and we'd take a huge picnic with us, or go out for a meal. There would always be plenty of eating and laughing as Dad squashed a week's worth of parenting into one day.

The renovations on the new restaurant began quickly, and to this day the smell of plasterboard and paint still reminds me of that building. When I recall the interior of the restaurant, I realise that Dad was quite *en vogue* for the time. The walls were covered in wet plaster and left to dry without smoothing, leaving a raised and lumpy finish. The carpets were deep burgundy, with brass separators at the entrance to each door. The skirting boards and woodwork were painted a deep brown and the ceilings were fitted with electric, three-blade fans. The tablecloths were cream and brown and every setting had its own chopstick holder, something new for its time. The dining space was just big enough for eight tables, which made it feel very much a small, family-run place where you could be sure of a warm welcome.

I was old enough to understand the challenge my dad had taken on, and I was excited. It was a huge risk for him, as he had invested all his savings in the business, but he was making a new life for his family so it was a risk worth taking. He was a proud and focused man, energised by possibilities and visions of what could be. I can clearly see characteristics in myself that I have obviously inherited from my dad: determination, drive, obsession, fear of failure and a need to be the best. Thanks, Dad!

The Panda was to be a restaurant like no other in Leicester. The other Chinese restaurants and takeaways that had opened since my grandfather's meant there was plenty of competition, but Dad had already established himself with the local residents and business people as a respected restaurateur. Now, he devised a new dining-out experience. No longer would customers have to choose from a 'chop suey' menu of noodles or steak and chips; now, they could experience the wonderful world of Chinese cuisine à la carte, courtesy of Mr John Wan.

Dad had moved the menu on a step from The Bamboo House and suddenly Chinese food was available in Leicester that had never been seen before: seaweed, kung pao, shark's fin soup ... this was all new, exciting, and people were keen to try it. It was obvious that The Panda was not destined for extinction when the restaurant opened, and rapidly became a roaring success.

To celebrate the new start, Dad threw an opening party and invited his loyal customers from The Bamboo House, some of whom had become our friends. I was at the party and it was here, for the first time, that I realised how physically different I'd become over the last couple of years. I still remember exactly how my sister looked that night: her hair was cut into a neat bob and she wore a black-and-red shift dress with an Aztec print, flat pointed shoes and a black-and-red plastic necklace of octagonal pieces that overlaid and formed a chain round her neck. She looked grown-up, beautiful and confident.

By contrast, I was no longer the cute chubby boy my father would parade in his restaurant or who would clamber on to the customers' knees – I had grown in height and mass into an overweight twelve-year-old on the brink of young adulthood. My cheeks were round and full, making my eyes sink into my face and almost disappear, and I had a wonky-fringed pudding-bowl haircut that was too young for me. My fingers had grown fat so that my knuckles dimpled and my legs had become thick but not like an athlete's; rather, they were like two spits of doner meat in a kebab shop. My stomach had stretched and an apron of flesh was forming above my trousers, while my chest had expanded, too, but not like a muscled warrior's – it was rounded, with the beginnings of fatty boobs, and my skin was tight under the pressure of my weight gain, almost as if my body had swelled quicker than my skin could grow. That day at the party, I realised I was fatter than my brother and sister.

We had always been a big family but I was the youngest and therefore I had always been the smallest. This new realisation was therefore extremely unfair. The others were older than me so I felt they should have continued growing – maybe a stone for every year of their lives, like I had done – but I had overtaken them. I was now the fattest of the fat family Wan.

I also realised on the day of the party that Oilen didn't look fat any more. She had lost her baby weight and slimmed into a beautiful lady. It was as if that day she went from being a girl to becoming a woman. She was then everything I wanted to be. But I was not sophisticated and grown-up like Oilen; I was fat, uncomfortable and embarrassed. For the first time, I was ashamed of how I looked.

When my mother had married my father, she had adopted his culture immediately and wholeheartedly. Even though Dad had made a life for himself in the West, he'd brought many of his Chinese traditions, rituals and superstitions with him, and they formed a major part of our upbringing. Our house was decorated with Chinese emblems; there were mirrors facing windows; and we burned joss sticks at the door, all of which was quite far out in Leicester in the seventies and early eighties. Dad's brothers had followed him over from Hong Kong and the family had all come to Leicester, setting up restaurants and takeaways. We'd meet up with our Chinese relatives for festivals and family celebrations such as birthdays and one-month parties (Chinese babies do not leave the house until they are one month old and a party is held to celebrate). Mum was adamant that we learn all the Chinese traditions and insisted we follow all the rituals, from Chinese New Year to burning pretend paper money for our ancestors and offering a suckling pig. We still do it, and I love all that now, and relish my Chinese heritage.

Dad wanted us to learn Chinese as well, but he was far too busy to teach us. It was, in fact, more practical for him to learn English, so that's what we spoke at home. Instead, when we were young, we went to Chinese school on Saturday mornings, but all I used to do was sit under the table and look up the girls' skirts (I know, surprising, isn't it?) and generally be naughty and disruptive. The only reason we went at all was because we were bribed with sweets and crisps to eat on the way home.

It was Dad's Chinese culture that stressed the importance of food and eating. In his culture, it was impossible to overfeed someone. The more food you gave someone, the more you were showing your love, and we were urged to eat all the time, without restraint. The bigger we got, the more loved we felt.

From the time it opened I helped out in The Panda, and I can see now how I learned how important it is to make someone feel comfortable, welcomed and appreciated. I realised how it was vital to understand how someone was feeling, and how to make sure they were looked after properly and cared for. Those were the skills I learned night after night, week after week, and year after year at The Panda.

Working in the restaurant was great. I got a small wage and I enjoyed being round the hustle and bustle of the customers. The weekend staff was usually made up of friends of my sister working to earn their own pocket money, and there was never time to be lonely. I became a familiar face to many of the regulars, and they greeted me with open arms and big smiles. It made me feel important, and I was happy.

One of my first jobs was working in the cloakroom. I greeted customers as they came in, taking their coats and giving them a small raffle ticket in return. I ticked off their names in the book and then escorted them into the bar. From there, my mum and dad would work their magic. Mum – behind the bar with her eighties perm – was the timid one, but that seemed to work in their well-rehearsed double act. Dad was a showman. He always knew the customers' names and welcomed them in to the restaurant as if it was his home. Once they were seated, he'd begin his performance, smiling broadly, clapping his hands together and saying, 'Let me feed you!' The regulars knew what was coming, while new customers would sit intrigued and delighted as Dad freestyled through the menu, conjuring up a delicious and varied feast.

With the meal ordered, it was my turn to play a role in the family circus. I would dart over from my post at the entrance, armed with a small duplicate pad, and take their wine order. It was a very important job, you know! I took it very seriously, and often recommended a wine: 'Have you tried the house white? Excellent with the chicken that Dad suggested. Or perhaps you'd prefer a red? I hear the Côtes du Rhône is very good.'

I cringe now when I think back to it, as I was no more than twelve when I was advising our customers which wine to drink. I obviously had no idea what I was talking about but working in the restaurant gave me the confidence to become my father's son. The customers would usually go with my suggestion out of sheer politeness and it wasn't long before I had worked out this was a sure-fire way to sell the most expensive wines.

I got my training by watching my parents as well as my sister. Oilen had been a waitress in the restaurant from its opening. She was good with the customers because she knew the game: when to speak, when to serve and when to rush in and clear the dishes. The customers liked her and she knew how to talk to them. While Oilen could chat away fearlessly, I didn't have that sort of confidence and I'd rely on my smile to win over the customers.

Kwok-Lyn didn't want to work the front of house so he helped in the kitchen and washed dishes. In his white chef's apron and tracksuit, he hauled huge, stainless-steel containers of dirty dishes, his brow sopping with sweat under the intense heat of the boiling water, but he never complained.

There we were, the whole family, each performing their own special act.

'Roll up, roll up! The one and only Family Wan Circus!'

Salt Fish Fried Rice

INGREDIENTS

One-day-old cooked white rice
4 eggs, beaten
Peas
Spring onions
Dried salt fish
Fish sauce
Salt and pepper
Soya sauce
Vegetable oil

METHOD

Heat a wok with 4–5 tablespoons of vegetable oil. When the oil begins to smoke, add the peas and spring onions and fry for 30 seconds. Now add the beaten egg and salt and pepper. Scramble the egg for about 20 seconds. Once the egg has formed, add the cooked rice and stir furiously, ensuring the rice does not stick to the wok. Add the soya sauce and fish sauce to taste and crumble in the dried salt fish. Toss for a further 2 minutes and then serve in a big round bowl and decorate with more chopped spring onions. Eat, enjoy and make sure you have time for a lie-down afterwards.

CHAPTER THREE

The Gok-arina Years

Inside the family and in the restaurant, I felt safe. Outside was a different matter. The Wan family stood out in a sea of white faces. There was my Chinese dad, my big, apron-wearing English mum, and three fat, mixed-raced kids. We came in for torrents of abuse whenever we set foot outside the front door. My mum was stopped in the street and told that the children she was pushing in her buggy couldn't possibly be hers. Us kids were called names and told we were half-breeds.

In many ways, the abuse simply bounced off us. As a family unit, we were strong, like a bowl of noodles, each ingredient strengthening and creating the dish, making it a whole. As long as I was immersed inside my solid, close-knit, loving family, I was protected. But once I was away from them, and as I got older and became more aware of myself, I discovered my vulnerability.

My first school was Barley Croft Primary School, a single-storey building in the heart of Beaumont Leys. In its heyday, the school boasted about its facilities, which included a huge sports field and its own 'music studio'. (This was, in fact, just a box of tambourines and a piano kept in a tiny room dedicated to music.)

I enjoyed primary school and was happy there. It was fun; I liked the teachers and there was no bullying. For one thing, I was bigger than most of the kids and they weren't going to bully me – if anything, I was probably more frightening to them. I was an average student, happy to get on with my work and neither outstandingly good nor outstandingly bad.

Not long after I arrived at school, the headmaster gave a talk on Chinese New Year, and Oilen, Kwok-Lyn and I were called out to sit at the front. It was one of the proudest moments of my life, thinking that I had something special that no one else had. Even though I didn't say or do anything, it felt like a performance and I enjoyed the feeling of everyone's eyes on us.

At school, I found I had a natural empathy with girls and women. I would surround myself at school with colourful and interesting girls, and I was always more interested in drawing and skipping than in playing football or running round the playground. I would play with the girls' hair, suggesting partings or carefully braiding their ponytails. I evaluated the teachers' outfits – 'I like Mrs Clark's dress; she looks pretty' or 'Mr Merton's trousers are too short, you can see his socks.' The girls always listened and agreed with me, which made me feel great, and while I filed all that away for much later, it was a kind of apprenticeship in looking at people and understanding who they were from their clothes.

I guess I knew from very early on that my world would be filled with the opposite sex. I believe that it's more than simply being gay. Gay is a bedroom choice and so, at the age of six, I don't think it determined the company I chose to keep: I barely knew I had a penis, let alone that I wanted to use it with boys! The boys always seemed unbearable with their knee-high attitudes and scruffy arrogance. The girls were always so much calmer. They reasoned, listened and – if I'm not misled by my rose-tinted glasses – they allowed me to feel special. By being the only boy in the group, I was able to shine and stand out. I never would have been able to that with the boys; I would have become just another playground statistic.

Even the female teachers seemed to understand me more. One of my teachers at primary school was Miss Richards, a tall and beautiful woman who can't have been more than twenty-eight. She always wore a neutral palette of nudes and flesh tones, her skin was golden brown all year round and her hair perfectly matched her skin with its honey highlights and caramel base. Miss Richards was kind and warm, tactile and soft, and she would never shout like the other teachers.

At 3 p.m. each day the class would close their work books, tidy their drawers and pack away their toys and then group on the carpet in our form space. Miss Richards would sit on an orange plastic chair and begin to read the 'end of day' story. I would race to the front of the class to take my prize of the seat on the floor closest to her chair. There I would smooth my hand down her legs as she read, the soft and warm nylon of her tights filling my entire body with comfort and satisfaction. Her gentle voice mesmerised me as she read stories with perfect pace and expression. At that chair I could imagine being Burglar Bill discovering Betty in his house, or living in a windowless house with the sinister Twits. I know it may sound weird and I am quite sure the authorities would have something to say about it in this day and age, but to my young and innocent mind it was perfect.

I was obsessed from an early age with organisation and accessories. I loved bags, pencil cases and new text books. Each term, we were all given salmon-pink work books, filled with lined, cotton-wool-coloured paper and pale-blue margins. There was something very satisfying about opening the cover of a new work book. I still love the smell of a new book – so clean and unused. My taste in accessories was practical and chosen for organisation rather than for the latest Superman design. I wanted pencil cases that kept my pencils neat and tidy, not slung in the bottom of my bag. I liked to write neatly in my exercise books and not spoil them with scribble and mess. I practised writing my letters so that the 'K' of my full name was perfectly formed, strong and majestic, while the 'y' curled down just right, below the line. With my head bent over so that my nose was almost touching the page, I would write slowly and carefully, marking out my own private territory.

I enjoyed projects, particularly making and decorating things, and I loved art and craft, even though I wasn't very good at drawing. But I had an eye for colour and how to make things look nice. I always put a lot of effort into appearances and how things looked.

After my starring role at the Chinese New Year assembly, I began to enjoy the spotlight and performing, even though I was thrown out of the school choir for being so bad at singing and demoted to banging a triangle, much to my mortification. I enjoyed entertaining people and it came easily to me. When I was about seven, my sister would dress me up in a pink tutu and I would run from one side of the house to the other on my tiptoes, pretending to be a 'Gok-arina'. It hurt my feet so much that even the memory of it makes my toes ache, but the pain didn't matter because I was being noticed.

It wasn't long before I started to crave the attention. I loved everyone looking at me and I'd cry when it was time for me to change out of my ballerina's costume. For years Oilen teased me, saying this was a clear indication of me being gay, but I think it was more about performing.

When I was eight years old, Mum would make Kwok-Lyn and me stand in the middle of the busy restaurant wearing matching outfits and sing 'Twas on a Starry Night'. Even though I sometimes grumbled that it was embarrassing, I secretly loved it and felt wonderful when we won a round of applause from the adults, and they smiled and said how cute we were.

As I began to grow up and become more aware of the world, the person who began to have the most influence over me was my older sister, Oilen. I guess it was hard for her, being the oldest child in our family. Our home life was hectic and unconventional, and because Mum and Dad were always very busy with the restaurant, Oilen had a lot of responsibility and often had to look after us younger ones. As a result, she became the adult in my life, the person who reasoned, advised and, in many cases, taught me how to grow. A huge responsibility for someone just four years older than me! But to me, Oilen always seemed to know so much. At school she was the only Anglo-Asian and she had to be very tough to handle it. She was picked on, like most kids, but she was never badly bullied, partly because she knew her own mind and wasn't afraid of telling people what she thought. She was strong and always seemed in control of her relationships with other people – in short, she was nothing like me. I was constantly unsure of myself and always seeking approval, and no one's approval mattered more than Oilen's.

To me, Oilen was beautiful, with big, round, brown eyes like bowls of melted chocolate, and thick glossy hair that perfectly framed her heart-shaped face. She was feminine and petite, unlike me with my large features, gargantuan frame and oversized everything. Like all of the Wan family, she had her struggles with weight, but I never saw her as anything other than fabulous. I used to creep into her lilac bedroom when she wasn't there, lie on her bed with her dusky pink-jacketed copy of *Little Women* and pretend to be her.

Oilen's tastes formed mine – she loved Abba, Eurythmics and Roxy Music, so I did, too (so much so that I chose 'Thorn in My Side' and 'Jealous Guy' as two of the eight tracks to take to my island when I appeared on Radio Four's *Desert Island Discs*). She took me into Leicester to buy my very first record, Billy Joel's 'Uptown Girl'. Oilen was also heavily responsible for my love of clothes. As she grew up, she began to play around with her style. It was the height of the New Romantics and the trends were androgynous and über glam. Men were wearing make-up and ruffles and their hairstyles were big and outrageous. The girls were provocative in men's tailoring, puffball skirts, stripy tights and carefully blended eye shadow in every colour of the rainbow. Oilen wore an outfit of a black tube skirt, black tights and an oversized, grey, men's suit jacket. She tied her hair back in a messy ponytail and knotted her fringe into a huge quiff, finishing it off with enormous silver hoop earrings. I loved my sister in this outfit: it was cool and contemporary, and she seemed to change her personality when she wore it, oozing confidence and appearing so in control of her space.

I was fascinated by the power of clothes. Long before I knew what body shapes were or how to accessorise an outfit, I began to see clothes as more than simply pieces of cloth that covered you up for decency's sake. I saw that they changed not only your personality but how people responded to you. They expressed the parts of your personality you wanted to reveal. They gave you the ability to be different. I wanted to dress with style and panache myself, but it was impossible – I was still just a little kid, and anyway, my body was beginning to swell out of all proportion to my age and it was comfort and practicality that had to take precedence. I was in baggy trousers and huge t-shirts; gorgeous outfits were banished to my fashion fantasies.

Oilen was such a huge influence in my life I would have done pretty much anything to be with her or, better still, be like her. One day, she picked me up from school, something she often did as Mum and Dad would be resting between their split shifts of lunch and dinner trading. Oilen was with her motley crew of classmates, all girls, dressed in their royal blue school uniforms with socks at half-mast. One of her friends was talking about the events of the day and she called one of the teachers a pervert. I couldn't have been older than nine and I clearly remember this new word fascinating me. How grown-up and thoroughly fabulous was this word – *pervert*! Oilen and her friends were so mature and sophisticated compared to me, with their casual use of words I didn't understand. I listened as hard as I could without understanding what they were talking about. Marching behind my sister's gang, I began to shout at the top of my voice: 'I'm a pervert … Hello, I'm a pervert … Nice to meet you, I'm Pervert … How do you do? … Pervert's the name.' My sister and her friends swung round in absolute amazement but, as all teenagers would, they simply burst into fits of laughter at the stupidity of Oilen's younger brother. I misunderstood their laughter for praise and basked in the attention, shouting 'I'm a pervert!' even louder, thinking it would make them like me when really it just made it obvious how young and silly I was.

I longed to be accepted by Oilen and her friends, but, of course, they had their own lives to live and Oilen didn't want to be bothered by her annoying little brother. For years, while she was going through puberty and adolescence and I was just a kid, she pushed me away. She would sit in her bedroom with her friends 'girl talking', and I was never allowed in, or she would walk ahead of me with her school friends and I was made to walk far enough away that I couldn't hear what they were saying. I wanted to belong so much. Once, when they were all in the kitchen, I came running in and offered to help make their sandwiches. 'All right, then,' Oilen said, 'You do it.' And they all marched out, leaving me alone to get on with it. (I can still feel that rejection while writing this!)

I understand completely why all those incidents happened and I don't blame her for it, but it was hard at the time when all I wanted was her acceptance and approval. I always had her love, though, and I knew that she was looking out for me.

Meanwhile, Kwok-Lyn and I – close in age and still similar in mannerisms – shared a bedroom, which made us comfortable in each other's company (it wasn't until Oilen went to university that I finally got my own space). I always felt strong when I was with my brother. He accepted me as I was, completely unconditionally. He never judged me, as Oilen sometimes did; he never told me what I had to do, as Mum and Dad did; and he never teased me, as kids at school did. Kwok-Lyn was my best friend, but it took me a very long time to realise it.

Kwok-Lyn always had a very close relationship with Mum. Oilen and I would tease him, calling him 'Mummy's Boy' and 'God-Lyn'. We knew it wasn't favouritism; it was just that he simply needed Mum's support more than we did. As in many Chinese families, as the oldest son he carried huge responsibilities and expectations. Dad wanted, and still does, 'God-Lyn' to be the one to take over the business, be our family's representative and be the child who makes all the right choices – there's never room for failure or mistakes if you're the eldest boy! This must have been a great pressure for Kwok-Lyn and I think Mum was particularly protective towards him because of it. It's a pressure I would not have welcomed.

The year I began secondary school was the same year Oilen left to go to college to sit her A levels. I sometimes wonder if my time at school would have been different if Oilen had been there with me, and whether she could have protected me from what was waiting round the corner, but I'll never know. As it was, there was only one week when we overlapped at 'big' school.

The summer before I moved to secondary school, all the new students attended an induction week to our new hell, Babington Community College. It was terrifying but I was also excited at the thought of spending more time with Oilen and Kwok-Lyn: I imagined that they dominated events there as much as they did at home, particularly Oilen with her quick mind and strong personality, and I assumed I'd see them all the time. Things proved to be very different from what I'd expected, however.

The week was extremely busy, run with timetables, assemblies and, of course, lessons, and the newbies were kept well away from the more senior pupils. Every day I would search for Oilen at break and lunchtimes, hurrying through the huge school in search of my all-powerful sis, but she was nowhere to be seen. I was very disappointed but I understood that she was busy doing whatever the important older students had to do.

The induction week was horrendous. We had lessons in languages I had only ever heard on TV, we had timetables we had to stick to without prompts from the teachers, we were thrown into a room full of strange kids from other primary schools and then there was … P.E.!!!

All through primary school, I had managed to dodge P.E. almost entirely. Mum (always on my side rather than the school's) had become a genius letter writer and her elaborate excuses had fended off the teachers beautifully. I had managed to get through primary school without doing any formal exercise at all; nothing beyond running round the playground. But big school was a whole different ball game, quite literally, and I had a horrible feeling that I was not going to be able to avoid the dreaded physical education.

P.E. was like torture. As I'm sure you can imagine, any physical activity for someone bigger than the average person is like punishment for eating too much. And I looked so very different from all the other kids round me: my hair was jet-black and greasy, I had started to form the early stages of acne and I had grown into a rotund and unattractive fat kid. I was desperately ashamed and embarrassed by how I looked, and sports always reminded me how unfit and wobbly I was.

I had heard horror stories from my brother and sister about P.E.: open changing rooms, five-mile cross-country runs and the dreaded communal showers. I hated my body so much, the very thought of changing in front of anyone made me sick to the very bottom of my stomach. The thought of being totally naked in a shower with 'normal' kids made my face hot, my mouth dry, my head hurt and my pulse race. I was petrified of anyone seeing what lurked under my clothes.

On our first day, we were asked to fill out our new timetable. We were given printed sheets with a horizontal grid, the days and lesson times in the margins. Monday was fine: English, Science, French and in the afternoon Social Studies. Tuesday was okay: double Science, double Art and in the afternoon Drama. Wednesday ... FUCK! It was the thing I dreaded most. Wednesday afternoon was double P.E. As Mr Dunn read out the day's lessons and all the other students happily filled in their timetables, I was struck dumb. My hands began to shake and anxiety filled every part of my body. I was panicking: I wanted my mum to arrive right then, armed with one of her famous letters, and rescue me. I wanted her to say, 'It's okay, no one is going to make you do P.E. ... You DO NOT need to get in the showers with the other boys, you DO NOT need to get changed in front of the other boys ... Get your things, we're leaving.' But no one – not Mum or Dad or even Oilen – appeared at the door. I was at big school now and this was how it was run. It was my fate to do P.E. and no one could or would stop it.

Wednesday couldn't have come around any quicker: it was if someone had stolen two days of my life. It was the only thing on my mind: P.E. for breakfast, lunch and dinner. Wednesday morning's lessons flew by, and before I knew it the lunch bell was rung. In exactly forty minutes' time, I would be queuing up outside the boys' changing room, standing in line with my sports kit in my bag surrounded by twenty athletic boys, all desperate to compete against each other at football or rugby or basketball. And then they would all happily joke and laugh as they stripped naked and showered, T.O.G.E.T.H.E.R., without a fucking care in the world ...

My life was about to end and, as I neared my death, there was no one around to save me. I spent the lunch break alone, watching the hands on my watch tick by as panic rose inside me. I roamed from corridor to corridor, from playground to classroom, in search of escape.

Moments before the afternoon bell rang, I found myself at the main reception to the school, where the receptionist sat behind her window, busying herself with trays of papers. It was then that the pressure combusted inside my young fat body. I felt a warmth round my legs and I realised that I was wetting myself. Before I could stop it, the pee came rushing out and although I was filled with the relief of letting go, I began to shiver with a combination of fright, mortification and cold. I was embarrassed beyond belief as I stood sodden with pee, paralysed by fear and self-hatred. Then the afternoon bell rang and I managed to walk to the receptionist's window and inform her I had 'made a mess'. She looked shocked and disgusted as she called my mum. 'Your mother is on her way to collect you,' she informed me from behind her window, her voice cold with disapproval. 'You can wait here. DO NOT sit on any of the chairs!'

I stood wet, cold and humiliated in reception until Mum arrived. The school corridors were silenced by the afternoon's lessons and a fear rose in me that behind every closed classroom door the only subject on the teachers' and students' minds was the fat, smelly boy in reception who was covered in 'mess'.

I don't know to this day if I wet myself out of fear or if I knew it was the only way I would get out of revealing my naked body. It only put off the inevitable – I would end up having to suffer the torment of the changing rooms and P.E. every week, anyway. It was clear, though, that my weight was beginning to dictate how I ran my life.

On the last day of the induction week, I finally found Oilen. It was hot as we stood at the back of the sports hall in the playground and, as I stared up at her, the sun blinding me, Oilen told me that I had to look after myself at secondary school and that if people called me names or bullied me, then I would need to stand up for myself and shout back at them.

But what neither of us knew was that my time at secondary school was to be the beginning of years of suffering.

CHAPTER FOUR

Cable-knit Forcefield of Fashion

By the age of eleven, I realised that I was fat. I'd gone to primary school as a chubby little kid and grown bigger as I discovered my love of food. I even loved school dinners.

Mum had always refused to cook English food at home and on the rare occasions that she did, it was horrible. Her chips were not good but I was the only one of us who pretended to like them as it was worth the oily, bland taste if it stopped Mum being upset. So at home, we always ate Chinese food. I even forced myself to like lychees, which I'd hated at first, because Dad would bring them home for us all and I didn't want to miss out on what Oilen and Kwok-Lyn were having. I loved English food, though, especially if it was done right, and I thought

47

school dinners were delicious, stuffing away as much as they would let me have. In fact, all three of us adored chicken fricassee so much that Mum went up to the school to find out the recipe (I bet she was the only mum doing *that*).

As council estate kids, we were also given free milk, which I thought was yummy. And then there had been the Aladdin's Cave at primary school – the tuck shop. A veritable smorgasbord of delights, the tuck shop was an irresistible lure. Under the pretence that I wanted to 'help' there, I managed to steal bags and bags of my favourite Worcester-sauce-flavoured crisps. Besides crisps, I loved chocolate and sweets (although nothing too chewy that took ages to eat – cramming it all in as quickly as possible was the main thing).

Events in our lives still continued to be marked by food, and we thought about what we were eating or what we were going to eat most of the time. Dad wanted us kids to do karate and, a bit like the situation with the Chinese lessons, the only way we could be persuaded to go was with the promise of a bucket of Kentucky Fried Chicken afterwards. That's my main memory of karate – not the outfit or the jumping around, but the half-crispy, half-soggy, intensely savoury oiliness of fast-food chicken. Food made me feel warm, comfortable and happy. But there was big trouble brewing in little China.

*

Not even food could help me with secondary school. Right from the start, I found it extremely difficult to cope with secondary school. I felt like an outsider: I was not academic, I was fat, I was mixed race and I was clearly different. I was the only one who went home to a restaurant and who spent my weekends working. And, as I grew up, I was beginning to realise that my sexuality was not like the other boys', and they sensed that, too. I was a ripe target for bullies – who better to pick on than the fat, queer Chinese boy? All at once, the safety and security I'd had at primary school was ripped away and the harsh coldness of secondary school came as a horrible shock.

At first, I was just ignored, like the other uncool kids. I hung out with the oddballs like me who were considered beneath the dignity of being noticed by the popular crowd, but they were friendships of convenience rather than truly heartfelt. We only stuck together because there was no one else, and we hoped there would be safety in numbers.

Despite my few friends, I felt isolated and terribly lonely, and I really was beginning to hate the way I looked. As puberty and adolescence slapped me round my big face, I began to grow, and by the time I reached the age of thirteen I was nearly six foot. I was grossly overweight and although I don't know exactly how much I weighed at this point, it was certainly over twelve stone; I was larger than most adults I knew. On top of that, my skin had erupted with spots and I still had that jet-black, greasy hair. In short, I considered myself the most unattractive person in the world.

I used to daydream about how I would look if I had the magical powers to transform myself. I would be slim and good-looking, and have a flat chest with pecs instead of small breasts. I'd have a taut stomach with a neat little belly button right in the middle, instead of one lost deep within rolls of flesh. My hands would be strong and lean instead of chubby, my hair would be dark blond and I would have clear, pink skin and wide, engaging eyes instead of slits of nothingness.

I was desperate to feel attractive and fit in. But with every year that passed, it got worse. There was no uniform at Babington and I wore the only clothes that were comfortable for me: M&S tracksuits with elasticated waists that were too short for my long legs. They marked me out even more as different, and I hated them. They were ugly and made me feel even uglier for wearing them. They felt like a prison uniform, but instead of arrows I had bad stitching.

With every day that went by, my self-esteem plummeted further, and my lack of confidence made me a sitting target for the bullies. It began gradually, but once it started it grew in intensity, and it came from every direction. The bullying was not Hollywood-style stuff; it didn't take the form of punches or kicks or physical violence, and maybe it would have been easier to cope with if it had. But I was tall and there was enough of me to make even the toughest bully think twice about taking me on physically. The bullying wasn't even particularly public. If it had been, I think that would have been easier to bear because I could have turned it into a performance and perhaps even been able to fight back in some way. It didn't even come from one or two loudmouths. It was more insidious and clever than that. It was a constant drip-drip of whispered insults, of quiet little sneers, a stream of mockery and name-calling, and it seemed that everyone was at it. The teachers appeared to notice nothing; it was as though only I could hear the secret voices filling the classrooms, the corridors and the dining hall with an endless litany of derision. And while there weren't the theatrical punches, comedy bag-snatchings or fat-boy sprawlings of bullying cliché, there were the tiny pinches, pokes and kicks that came from everywhere – as I stood in the dinner queue or outside a classroom waiting for lessons. They were miniature attacks, too small to report or complain about, but cumulatively painful and demoralising. It was teenage psychological warfare and I was powerless against it, with no way to respond. All I could do was listen until the words echoed constantly in my mind and I began to believe they were right: I was stupid, worthless, fat, ugly, greedy, gay ...

The bullying was isolating because no one else seemed to notice it was happening, and I didn't want to discuss my humiliation with anyone. I was afraid of telling my family because they had problems of their own.

Many other Chinese restaurants had opened in Leicester, all copying the formula my father had created. The late eighties was also the beginning of the downturn, and as the recession took hold people stopped spending money in restaurants. We were no longer the dining-out hot spot, the there were no more full columns in the reservation book.

Dad was beginning to feel the strain and I had started to worry about my parents' health. They always seemed so tired and they never had any time for themselves; away from the restaurant, all their energies were poured into their children. We never had holidays like most families because there was never a good time to close the business. The only time my parents didn't work was on the occasional trip to my nan's, my maternal grandmother, and that was never for longer than two or three days.

So by the age of thirteen, I was exhausted – I was in full-time school and my weekends were spent working in the restaurant. Our family life was dominated by The Panda and it seemed like we were the hardest working family in the city, but I knew it was a matter of our survival.

How selfish would I be to tell them I was miserable when they were dealing with a failing business and struggling to keep their heads above water? I didn't try to fight against the bullying, as there didn't seem any way to defend myself. Instead, I tried to endure the taunts: 'queer', 'fatty', 'bender', 'batty boy', 'faggot', 'stupid'; but they wore me down, destroying my confidence and making me hate myself.

Life became an endless trial as I put up with the awful treatment meted out to me by the kids who didn't know how lucky they were to be 'normal'.

The only tactic that I could think of to stop all this was to please the bullies and make them my friends, so I began taking the piss out of myself. Soon, self-deprecation became a part of my act. I figured that if I took the piss out of myself first, then it would stop the bullies from getting to me. I thought I had found a way to arm myself and that this invisible shield of self-hatred was bully-proof – but of course it wasn't; it just gave them more reason to pity me and intensified their mockery.

It wasn't just in school that people felt able to jeer at me or make comments about my appearance. Being fat and eating in public is like a forbidden sin. How dare a chubby person possibly do the one thing that makes them evil, greedy and antisocial ... EAT? Sometimes it felt as if consuming cakes and burgers on the streets of Leicester was on a par with touching and kissing in public in certain Middle Eastern countries – an arrestable offence.

One day, when I was almost thirteen, I was walking from the corner shop back to my house. I had been to collect a paper for Dad and as payment for my journey I had treated myself to a Cadbury's Flake.

The first bite was amazing, but just as I swooped in for the next creamy and crumbly mouthful, a loud horn ripped through the air, so loud in fact that it managed to stop me mid-bite. A dirty, old, white van was driving past me and, hanging from the passenger window, was a builder decorated in dust, paint and a smug grin. It was his horn that had disturbed my chocolate fix. Not content with making the entire street aware of his presence, he went on to yell from his wank-mobile: 'Oi, oi, you fat bastard! 'Ave a salad!'

I was confused, my mind still on the pleasure of the chocolate bar and, not really understanding what was happening, I smiled, raised my hand and waved at the bastard! As the van bowled into the distance and I realised what I had done, I was nailed to the pavement with hurt and embarrassment, feeling disgusting to myself and everyone else around me. It was years before I could feel comfortable eating outside again.

Finally, after two years of ceaseless bullying, I realised that there was something I could do about my situation. During the summer of 1987, when I was thirteen, I asked Mum to take me shopping.

I had no idea then, but I was about to perform my very first makeover.

We went to Next (in those days a rather glamorous place to go shopping) and bought a cream cable-knit jumper, a pair of beige chinos and a pair of brown suede brogues. I also had my hair cut. I asked for a huge kiss curl that would hang perfectly to the left of my face and, with enough gel and teasing, it did. My makeover was complete.

I had not lost weight and I was certainly not happy with my body, but I felt different. I felt attractive and cool and, for the first time, confident away from The Panda. It was my first personal experience of the power of clothes to alter emotions and bestow confidence – something I had only seen, and envied, in other people up until then.

The first day back at school was incredible. I remember feeling nervous but excited about showing off my new look. Something inside me was different. I felt somehow stronger.

When I work with charities now that help children who are being bullied, I have one piece of advice: you have to be stronger than the bully. Bullies are clever. They will make you believe it is your fault. They will make you feel alone and, if they are really good at the job, they will make you feel as if you deserve it. But you have the power to say 'No' to that. It is your right. When you stand up for yourself, bullies will wonder if you are worth the trouble of tormenting, because they only victimise you if they can hurt you, as they enjoy the power that comes from seeing someone else suffer. If you show that they are not affecting you, the bullying will stop.

In a strange way, I think I knew this back then. My new look was never going to stop me from being fat or camp and if the bullies wanted to carry on taunting me, then they would. But I would be different when they did. I had my new suit of armour and as long as I felt good about myself, they could never harm me. To me, that cable-knit jumper was somehow like a superhero costume. And it worked. I walked into my form room and although I can't remember the reactions of the students, it must have been good. Within days, the name-calling was down to the odd 'Faggot!' in the corridor or the occasional 'Hubba Blubba' as I queued in the canteen, but I could deal with it.

I was no longer afraid to go into certain parts of the school in case I got held up like a side of meat to be devoured by some fifth-year barbarians. I held my head high and when the bullying happened, I just coped. Somehow my mind had adjusted and the name-calling mostly rebounded off my fat body. The words were the same but now they had different meanings. 'Fat' was somehow no longer insulting; it simply described what I obviously was – so how stupid were the bullies when they pointed out what was plain to see? It wasn't as though I felt the need to walk round the school making irrelevant statements like 'Piano ... teacher ... chair ... school fence.' My newfound confidence felt amazing. The ugly duckling had not turned into a swan but I was feeling great, and I began quacking as loudly as I could.

My transformation gave me the confidence I needed to make a new set of friends, which had secretly been my intention all along. In my superhero outfit, I found I could go up to people who would once have seemed out of my orbit. I could chat to them, crack jokes and try out a new personality to go with my new wardrobe. It worked. A group of girls quickly befriended me and it didn't take them long to forget that I had once been the subject of the school's taunts. It was as if I had never been the boy that had been snubbed, teased and pitied. It's strange how quickly we can forgive and forget: they extended their arms and welcomed me into their world, and I entered without hesitation.

I had always dreamed of this acceptance, thinking that if only I could be 'one of them' then my life would be wonderful. The popular kids seemed to have such great lives; they were happy in their skins and free from ridicule and persecution. I realise now that I was naive to believe they never felt sadness, rejection or loneliness but their outward appearance always led me to believe otherwise.

I enjoyed my new-found acceptance but it was bitter-sweet. I felt guilty for no longer being friends with the kids I was once bullied with. I would watch them struggle, and when the bullies attacked, see how they seemed to wilt and shrink down inside themselves, trying to avoid confrontation and the unnecessary taunts. My inner superhero would urge me to stand up for them, or for them to stand up for themselves, to find the strength to fight back – but they didn't. Instead they did what I had always done, moving round quietly, sticking together and being careful not to draw too much attention to themselves. I desperately wanted them to see the light and maybe reinvent themselves as I had that summer. But it was too hard now to stand up for them. One particular girl asked me why I no longer hung out with her. I told her that it wasn't about her, it was about me: I had to change because I had no choice. The bullying had been destroying me. I needed her to know I wasn't ashamed of our friendship, I was ashamed of who the bullies thought I'd been. Maybe she was stronger than me, maybe she knew this already. I can still remember the expression on her face: she looked hurt – but I knew she understood by the way she simply listened.

School is a hard place to be and when your chips are down it can be the loneliest place in the world. Perhaps I should have stayed with my original friends, and just borne the bullying. Maybe I was a coward for giving in to peer pressure to be like everyone else. Maybe I was a fraud and a fake. All I knew was that I had to change if I was going to make it.

Besides, something bigger was happening in my life. Deep down I knew I was gay, and it was going to take all my inner superhero to survive.

School Holiday Condensed Milk Sandwiches

INGREDIENTS

2 slices of white bread per person
Butter for spreading on the bread
Condensed milk

METHOD

Butter both slices of bread. Using a spoon or knife, coax the condensed milk on to one slice of buttered bread. It will want to escape, so you have to work quickly to spread it generously and evenly (not really possible) before placing the other slice of buttered bread, buttered-side down, on top of the gooey, sticky milk. Cut into 4 squares, leaving the crusts on, and eat messily, while generating sounds of appreciation for a true culinary masterpiece. This sandwich is best enjoyed sitting in the restaurant at lunchtime during the school holidays, waiting for Mum and Dad to finish the lunch service.

Recipe by: Oiley Boily on the Bum

CHAPTER FIVE

The Wan Within

Somehow, I had forced myself to change. I would not be the kid that everyone despised: I had undergone my very own makeover and it seemed to have worked. But I still needed to distract people from my weight and what I considered to be my ugliness, so I had begun to invent a new personality that used wit, humour and repartee to keep others from noticing my faults. This idea worked well, and it attracted people of a kind I'd never known before. They took me to new, untried paths with edgier thrills and the spice of the forbidden.

My new friends were dangerous and exciting. They were a mixed bunch of girls who ran their lives by a fascinating new set of rules. My old friends had been concerned with getting good marks in school, obeying their parents and staying out of trouble. These girls were cooler. They rebelled against the system. When the teachers said no, it was a clear instruction to do it. WOW!!!

There were three girls in particular – Soul, Rachel and Amy – who became my best friends. Many an evening was spent hanging out at the swings, or roaming the streets looking for entertainment, while we puffed away on cigarettes.

I had started smoking at about twelve years old. My dad smoked and he would stand at the front of the restaurant with his panda-shaped ashtray, exhaling clouds of smoke from his Rothmans cigarettes, and he always looked so cool to me. Sometimes he'd leave a cigarette burning in the ashtray while he went to serve customers, and I'd sneak some drags on it. It was revolting, of course, and I'd cough and splutter but I persevered because I wanted to be like my dad. It didn't matter that neither Oilen nor Kwok-Lyn smoked (although my brother did start at around sixteen). Dad would buy packets of Rothmans in 200-pack boxes and, before long, I had started nicking them. By the time I was thirteen, I was smoking properly, and so were all my friends.

I loved my new gang, feeling as though, at last, I belonged to something other than the restaurant. My mind was beginning to develop and I needed constant stimulation, something my new network gave me. We all shared the same sense of humour. I had learned that I didn't need to laugh at myself all the time; there were plenty of sources of jokes all round me. I started to come up with the gags, making fun of situations and other people instead of just myself, and I discovered that making people laugh was a powerful feeling. I enjoyed amusing my posse of cool girls and hanging out with them brought another bonus: they were good-looking birds, so there was never a short supply of boys that wanted to speak to us.

I'd known from an early age the way I felt about boys was different to how I felt about girls. Boys were mysterious and rude; they were naughty and intriguing. Girls were safe. I could speak with girls freely and we laughed at the same jokes. I was interested in the important things in their lives: friendships, family and, of course, their looks. I didn't really understand what it meant to be gay: I only knew that I was different from other boys. As far as I was concerned, 'gay' was a word used to insult or offend; it was a bad place where the freaks of nature lived, and naturally I didn't want that, so I decided that I wasn't gay – I was just attracted to boys like my best friends were.

But things weren't simple any more. I was thirteen, my hormones were bursting out all over the place and my physical attraction to boys was starting to dominate my fantasies. I wondered what it felt like to lie next to a boy, or to hold a boy's hand, play with his hair or even kiss him. Although these thoughts repulsed me because I was afraid of being gay, they were also exciting and they began to grow in strength until I could think about little else. But when I looked down at my body I despaired, because I looked so different from the other lads. Although I had a new style, I was still fat and also tall enough to tower over most of my peers and teachers. I had bulging cheeks of flesh and large, crooked teeth. My eyes were deep set and appeared piggy in the mass of fat on my face, and my double chin had become wobbling and jowly from the strain of years of weight gain. The other boys were so handsome and fresh looking – bastards! – and their bodies were svelte and toned. They were so much smaller than me, too, even the taller ones, and were quick and agile, unlike me with my clumsy plodding. They were beautiful, and I most definitely was not. Compared to them, I looked like Hagrid from *Harry Potter*. I fancied almost all of them, and felt jealous of their good looks and easy style – attraction wasn't enough, I wanted to be one of the boys, too. But I didn't confide in anyone: I buried all that well below my ample surface.

Many of the boys had begun to borrow clothes from their older brothers and were morphing into young men with gel in their hair. We had all entered the strange world of puberty and some boys even had the early stages of moustaches. Being half-Chinese and a member of the un-hairiest race in the world, this was something I would never manage to achieve.

Meanwhile, I had the security of my set of female friends and it was easy for me to take a keen interest in how the girls looked and who they fancied, and as I would never look like them there was no competition. I was able to watch the girls flirt, tease and sometimes even kiss the boys. I was one of the gang and because I was friends with the girls, the boys reduced the bullying. Why wouldn't they when I held the key to what they wanted?

Rachel and Amy were both confident and popular, but our leader was Soul (not her real name). She was one of the beautiful girls at school: bright, daring, funny and cool. She lived with her mum and two younger siblings in a house that was minutes away from the school, which made bunking off easier. Soul was a mixed-race beauty and, in my eyes, she had it all. Her mum was a modern, new-thinking parent who made no secret of her enjoyment of drink, parties and make-up. It always felt like summer in Soul's house: reggae would blare from the open windows, there was a constant stream of visitors and there were never any rules. Soul was allowed to make adult decisions, even though we were only thirteen. It was as if Soul's mum had waited thirteen years for her to grow up so they could be best friends.

I loved Soul's house, even though most of the walls had been left stained with alcohol from the parties; there was never soap or toilet roll in the loo; the small, council-house garden was overgrown and unkempt. The house might have needed a good airing, but it was exciting. There was always an open pack of B&H on top of the microwave, there was always company and the lack of rules meant that we could pretend we were in control of our own lives.

Like most teenagers, I was busy experimenting with things that made me feel grown-up. I tried the occasional spliff; I never really liked it because it made me lethargic and paranoid but when everyone was else was doing it, I joined in every now and then. We drank cheap alcohol – Mad Dog 20/20 and Diamond White – and I liked the way it made me feel brave and uninhibited. I'd grown up around booze, as food and drink always went together in the restaurant, and although my family weren't big drinkers, I soon enjoyed going out and having a drink as part of my socialising.

The more I hung out with the girls, the more my school-work suffered. My mindset had changed. I didn't have time for homework any more, and on many days even attending school felt like too much hassle. I was never the brightest student but so far I had worked hard in lessons and my marks were average. Besides, most of my old friends had been academically gifted and they had helped me with my work. This was something I could never have asked of my new friends – I had to be cool, no, the *coolest* – and asking for help would have blown my cover. As I flunked, lied and rebelled my way through my third year, I began to fall behind and my relationship with my teachers started to become tense and uneasy.

I had always respected the adults in my life and the teachers were no exception, but as I began to experience failure, I got myself a whole new attitude. My new friends' bravado was infectious and I was more confident and able to speak up where once I'd been quiet and biddable. The teachers no longer saw me as a pupil with potential; I was the loud, mouthy and disruptive kid who needed no encouragement. Deep down, I hated pissing the teachers off – I've always wanted approval from other people – but I started to enjoy the attention I got when I misbehaved. My classmates would laugh and cheer me on and, while they were laughing at what I was doing, they weren't laughing at *me* – it was survival.

I started to develop the knack of holding an audience long enough to set up a gag and execute a punch line bang on target. Whether I was taking the piss out of the teacher, back-chatting or being self-deprecating, I was getting laughs and this gave me a buzz I had never experienced before. It made me feel accepted and needed, and not like the bullied, fat, ugly boy I 'knew' I was. I now had a purpose in my new life, and that was to entertain.

I had taken drama as one of my third-year options because it was a sure-fire way of getting out of P.E., which I still loathed with a passion. Besides, my classroom cabaret was going so well that it seemed like a natural choice and I had a feeling I might be quite good at it. Thankfully I was right. Within a short space of time, Drama became the only subject I would never fail.

We had drama lessons on the stage in the school theatre, a dark space with black-painted walls, floor-to-ceiling black-out curtains and a state-of-the-art rigging loaded with spotlights and theatre lamps. My time in the drama studio is my happiest memory of school. The drama teacher was a youngish man called Steven Skidmore and he was creative, understanding and funny. I am quite sure that if my sexuality had been more developed, I would have had a huge crush on him but, fortunately for him, I was too concerned with being on stage to fall in love (a habit that has never quite left me!). The drama lessons were mainly practical and there were no right or wrong answers, unlike maths or English. Instead we were marked on how we presented ourselves and portrayed emotions and I enjoyed that – A- for sadness and A+ for really fucking depressed!

My turbulent behaviour outside the drama studio had become a guilty pleasure. I enjoyed being cool and a bit of a bad boy, but I knew it wouldn't be long before I'd be hurting my parents. I was getting into trouble, and when they found out my home life would be disrupted. Drama became my sanctuary. The lessons felt like home, somewhere I could hide, let go and be myself. I found it easy to get up and perform: I wasn't afraid of sounding too gay, I wasn't nervous about telling the class about how I felt, and it was the one place in my world where my fat, grotesque body didn't matter. It was where I found confidence in my personality instead of feeling ashamed of my physical appearance, where my character mattered more than my physicality.

Each year the school performed a Christmas play – these were always very ambitious, some even said over-ambitious for a council estate school (I think the local authority considered that students had more chance of leaving in the fifth year and being banged up for arson and drugs than becoming rising stars of stage and screen. I feel quite honoured I've proved the bastards wrong). The students would light, stage-manage, costume design and perform the show. This particular year our school was putting on *The Really Wild West Show*, a play written and devised by Mr Skidmore. It was set – not surprisingly – in the old west of America and was filled with saloons, spittoons, cowboys and overacting – mostly by yours truly. I was given the part of the preacher and he was a great character to play. He was loud, evil and a criminal, only interested in swindling his congregation under the guise of preaching about the Lord. I was given my own song written in the style of old gospel – half-spoken in a thick, midwest accent and half-screeched like a character out of *The Blues Brothers*.

This was a big moment in my life. It was when I fell completely in love with performing. Dressed in my preacher costume, I was given license to be somebody different. I wasn't alone and struggling, I wasn't fat and bullied, I wasn't ugly and gay ... I was the preacher and *'Hallelujah, ain't no love in the world gonna mess with the GOOD LORD!!!'*

Being the preacher was a safe place for me to hide from my failing studies, my sexuality, my family responsibilities and my fear of not being liked. Even though I was far happier with my new friends, I was still struggling to feel accepted and not entirely at ease with my role as a rebel – but being a part of a stage production made me feel as if I belonged.

We performed the show for three nights. It was amazing: the nerves, the tension, the audience – *darling*, what a heady gok-tail! I stood on the stage, screeching, shouting and singing my fat little heart out. The eager audience 'ooh'ed and 'ahh'ed at all the right places and halfway through my song they even belly-laughed at my take on evangelical preaching. I was hooked! Performing was to be my new addiction, my new love – my new food! I want to dine every night on a feast of love, adoration, applause and satisfaction.

If *The Really Wild West Show* had given me a love of the spotlight, then the next year's production was to show me yet another facet of my character. The play we put on in my fourth year was *Cinderella*, and I was given the role of Dandini, Prince Charming's queenie sidekick. Dandini was over the top and brash. He was loud and delivered quick one-liners that could floor anyone that got in his way. I fell totally in love with him.

Up until then, I'd always been embarrassed by my real-life Dandini persona, but all of a sudden I was directed to camp it up, be outrageous and NOT be anything like a boy. It felt liberating to play to the side of my personality I had tried so hard to keep secret and I let rip, making extravagant gestures and mincing about as hard as I could. My costume was a white shirt, a black scarf flung camply round my neck and a pair of black-and-white polka-dot trousers that were borrowed from a sixth former called Magda.

Magda was a larger-than-life character who had come to Babington to sit her A levels. I fell in love with Magda as much as I fell in love with Dandini. She was fearless, striding round the corridors and knocking aside anyone who got in her way with her size-20 body. She wasn't ashamed of herself or embarrassed to be looked at – instead she had dyed red hair and wore loud and attention-seeking colours. She played the evil stepmother in our production and would belt out her songs as if she was playing to the Royal Albert Hall. She owned the stage and there wasn't any power in the world that could stop her. Magda was the first experience I had of gay cabaret; like a drag queen, she was quick-witted and sharp. Her mind seemed to work faster than anyone else's and her big physical presence filled the stage, and my heart, to bursting point. She was quite simply fabulous. When I worried about playing an obviously gay character, I would watch her and think, *If she can do it, so can I!* I learned so much from her and one of the regrets I have is that I never realised it at the time so I could say thank you.

Thankfully, the audience loved Dandini. They took him to their hearts and cared for him each of the three nights he appeared. They adored his camp one-liners and laughed heartily at his outrageous behaviour, and when Prince Charming married Cinderella, they sympathised with his broken heart. Now, twenty years later, I know just how important Dandini is in my life. When I am on stage performing to thousands of people or even sometimes when I am with my closest friends, Dandini is re-born. He is sensitive, and happy to play the fool just as long as you know he, too, needs to be loved. He doubts Prince Charming will ever love him back but that's okay as long as the audience loves him instead. Dandini is no fool; he knows his place is playing the stooge rather than the handsome, charismatic prince, but his consolation will be a very special relationship with the audience.

Thanks to Dandini and Magda, I began to feel more comfortable with my gay identity. I accepted that I was gay and that at some point I would need to do something about it. I was also now convinced that acting was the one thing in life I could do, and I began to nurture dreams that I might be able to go on the stage ...

CHAPTER SIX

Fuck Exams!

My performances on the school stage and in Drama classes couldn't entirely save me, however. I was fifteen years old and defiantly adamant that I didn't see the point of school. Because I had made it quite clear that I had no intention of buckling down and doing any work, the school began to agree that there was no point in wasting my time and theirs. The teachers, tired of my attitude and my backchat, their patience exhausted by my disruptive behaviour and poor attendance, decided that I was a lost cause and gave up on me. As the summer exams approached, the school asked me to leave before I had chance to sit them. The local authority thought it a good idea to place me on 'extended work experience' in my dad's restaurant. (I don't know what they would have done if Dad had been unemployed – possibly placed me on an 'extended benefits experience'.)

That was it. I had flunked school and was leaving with no qualifications whatsoever. I found myself on a downward path to a life of failure, obscurity, poverty and, most likely, addictions of various kinds. It wasn't unimaginable. For every student like my sister Oilen, who studied, got to university and escaped into a good career, there were plenty who fell through the cracks. Some girls got pregnant too young, some got mixed up with drugs or bad boys who distracted them from their own futures. Plenty of pupils didn't think any kind of decent life was for them.

I was nearly one of them. Kwok-Lyn had managed to get to college, but I was shackled to the restaurant with a head full of dreams and an almost non-existent self-belief. Although I loved Mum and Dad and I was grateful they had given me a life, home and now a full-time job, The Panda was their dream, not mine. I resented the business. It had dominated my life – the whole of my life – and now I had to work there full-time because I had been told I was not clever or capable enough for school. I had become another statistic destined for a string of Youth Training Schemes and I was supposed to be grateful for having a job, any job, just as long as it kept me away from the school and off the streets.

I was deeply unhappy and confused. How could I have fucked up so badly? A small part of me regretted leaving my academic friends back in the third year. Maybe if I had remained unloved, bullied and teased, I would have worked hard and achieved something. At least then I would have been miserable with prospects. As it was, I felt hopeless. I had no qualifications, having been booted out of school, I had had to leave Dandini behind me, but my feelings towards boys were definitely not a phase ...

I was afraid to admit the fact that I was gay to myself, let alone to anyone else around me. I feared that if my family discovered I was gay, they would disapprove and perhaps reject me. My father was a traditional Chinese man in many ways, and in his culture, homosexuality simply wasn't recognised or spoken of. My being gay could be a source of shame for him and there was a chance he might feel that I could no longer be a part of the family. I was not prepared to take that risk. My family was all I had and the thought of them not being there to help me when I needed them was unspeakable, so my sexuality had to remain hidden.

But my 'dark secret' became increasingly hard to hide as I started to develop very adult crushes. My earliest major infatuation, when I was about thirteen, was with one of the waiters in Dad's restaurant – he shall be known as Blue Eyes. He was in his mid-twenties, tall, blond and the sexiest man I had ever seen. He was a fitness fanatic and would cycle hundreds of miles a week to and from the restaurant. I was obsessed with Blue Eyes. His body was grown-up and muscular, his cheekbones and jaw line were sharp and sculpted and his hair was perfectly floppy with natural honey-coloured highlights. He had a cheeky, boyish grin and when he smiled at me it was if I had discovered the happiest place on earth.

Blue Eyes would arrive each evening, hot and flushed from his Tour-de-Leicester ride. In the customer toilets, he would change out of his sweaty cycling gear into his work uniform of white shirt, tux trousers and black dickey-bow. You could guarantee I would always be in the toilet, waiting to catch a glimpse of him undressing. I feel quite sure he knew what I was doing; although he was happy with his girlfriend, he never asked me to leave and I am sure he would sometimes stand a moment longer in only his underwear, for my hormonal pleasure. It felt risky to do it but the excitement took control, and I figured if my peeping was challenged, I could explain it away. Fortunately for me, our daily 5 p.m. rendezvous were never exposed – and it also never blossomed into anything more than fuel for my fantasies.

Food was still a big presence and a big pleasure in my life. I had an enormous appetite and I satisfied it. Working in the restaurant meant that I was surrounded by food, so I ate constantly. Now that I was no longer at school, I was getting less exercise than before, but I couldn't stop eating. It was my drug, and I was constantly high on food. It filled my hours of boredom and gave me short-term happiness. By now, my body had grown even bigger and my weight had become an all-consuming issue. I was disgusted at how I looked and even showering was a painful and embarrassing task. I would run the hot water for at least ten minutes before getting undressed so that the bathroom mirrors would steam up and prevent me catching a glimpse of my fat body; it is something I still do now from habit. How could Blue Eyes, or anyone, possibly find me attractive if I couldn't even look at myself? But I had no idea how I could tackle my weight problem, or even if I really wanted to. After all, food was my only comfort in life.

As the months rolled by, I started to become unsettled and impatient at the restaurant. I was tired of working every night and weekend and not even my very adult thoughts about Blue Eyes were a big enough distraction. I felt as though my life was over, and I was still only fifteen.

I decided I needed to make something of myself. I knew the restaurant would never fulfil my ambitions so I began to look for something I wanted to do. I studied the Classifieds of the local paper, looking for work. In my heart I wished I could find an advert asking for a bright, young, gay actor to tour the world in a brand-new stage production, but instead it was column after column of home workers, sales people and the occasional skilled job – which I didn't have the skills to do.

By sixteen, I decided to go for a couple of jobs and soon it was my first day with a double-glazing company. The office was a small mobile unit made, believe it or not, of uPVC. There were six or seven tables in the office, ominously kitted out with a telephone each and a copy of the local telephone directory. At the end of the room there was another table for our team leader and next to it, on the wall, was a bell. The room was sterile and white, cold and soulless, as if the space had been constructed as an oversized coffin for dreams, hopes and laughter to go and die.

After a morning of being taught how to not ask 'closed-end' questions, learning the pricing and rehearsing our standardised greetings, we hit the telephones. Armed only with our directories and a dream of ringing the sales bell, we marched our way through every number in the book.

With each and every call I made, a small part of me died. I hated this job; it was thankless, boring, repetitive and the constant 'No!'s and 'Fuck off!'s were destroying my already shaky confidence. From my table I would stare at the dusty bell and think, *I don't give a shit about this, I hate double glazing, I don't know what uPVC stands for* – but to ring that bell would be like a life orgasm, so for a few weeks I persevered.

After a month, I could bear it no longer. Bruised and ashamed, I walked away from the uPVC unit in search of something better. And I never did get to ring that bloody bell.

Meanwhile, my dad's friend had opened a small café in a village just outside the city – I'll call it Café Hell and him Uncle A. My dad had suggested to Uncle A that he give me a trial since I had years of experience working in the restaurant, and I was good with the customers.

Café Hell was small and had been put to together on the cheap. The tables were covered in red-and-white gingham plastic tablecloths and the menu was basic and uncreative. The village was small, but other than a Gregg's Bakery, Café Hell had no real competition. I began working in the café and it wasn't long before I realised how lucky I had been to work in Dad's restaurant. His customers were lively and familiar, they were polite, grateful and always knew my name – in many ways, I realised Dad's customers had become a part of my extended family.

Café Hell couldn't have been more different. The customers were rude, ungrateful and kept themselves to themselves. They didn't want a chat and were not interested in what I thought; they simply wanted to be left alone with their jacket potatoes and measly slices of cash-and-carry cake.

Uncle A was married to a white woman, Auntie A. She was pretty, younger than my mum, and she smoked. Auntie A would work the tables with me while her husband cooked in the kitchen. All three of us would spend our days pouring, frying, slicing and wiping in Café Hell. It was monotonous and dull and, to add to the torture, Auntie A had an antisocial love for Shakatak. She would insist on playing the same album (possibly the only one they produced) over and over again at maximum volume – all fucking day long! She would sashay round the café in her nylon apron, wiping tables and clearing cups while humming along to FUCKING Shakatak! It was like having my head permanently trapped in an elevator, or like some kind of hideous military torture. My clothes stank permanently of cheap bacon, my hands were dry and cracked from all the washing-up, my brain had disintegrated and I had synth-style tinnitus. Café Hell made me realise that there was no way on earth I wanted my life to be like this, so after just a few weeks I asked Dad to make my excuses and I sloped back to the restaurant with my tail between my legs and a life-long allergy to Shakatak.

I was desperate not to wish my life away. I was working full-time in the restaurant again and trapped in a vicious cycle: my only comfort and happiness came from food, which in turn made me feel fat and miserable, feelings that could only be alleviated by eating. The only thing I could think about was being an actor. I would watch films and dream that one day I would be a handsome leading man. I made myself believe that if I could just get a break performing – the only thing I thought I was good at – I would suddenly be slim and handsome. And then it wouldn't matter if I were gay, because all people who work in the arts were gay; it was what gay people did. That was my only desire, my only dream. It was the only way I could see myself ever finding any happiness.

But I had to find a way to make my dream come true.

Mum's Scallop Congee

INGREDIENTS

1 cup of long-grain fragrant white rice
3 thin slices of raw root ginger
1 stem/leaf of preserved turnip
Approx. 3 pints of cold water
6 dried scallops (pre-soaked in hot water and broken
  into pieces once soft – save the liquid from soaking
  the scallops)
Soya sauce

METHOD

Wash the rice in cold water until the water runs clear. Drain. Put the rice in a large saucepan with the 3 pints of water. Bring to the boil. Once simmering, add the ginger, broken up scallops, turnip and water used to soak the scallops in. Continue to simmer for between 45–60 minutes or until the rice looks like a thick porridge. Add more water if you prefer a less 'stodgy' version. Or you can use a little less water at first and add more to achieve the consistency you prefer as the dish cooks. Serve in a big bowl with soya sauce to your taste. Warning: Looks like wallpaper paste but tastes like family love.

Recipe by: Momma Wan

CHAPTER SEVEN

A First Taste of Freedom

Working in my parents' restaurant, my uncle's café and attempting to sell double glazing had pushed me to a point of desperation. Although I was still fragile from school, I knew I had to grow up and stop being afraid of failing. So I took my chopsticks of determination, dug deep into my inner bowl and pulled out enough courage to consider going back into education. But this time I would be the one in control.

When I first walked into Charles Keene College in Leicester, I had no idea what to expect. I was nervous and unsure, but I knew this was what I had to do if I was ever going to become an actor. I had passion but I lacked the skills and confidence to make it, so I had no choice but to go in search of my dreams. The first step was to enrol at college.

As I walked through the courtyard outside the dance studio annexe's entrance, questions were racing through my head. Would the teachers be like the ones at school? Would they like me? Would they tell me I was too fat to be on the course? Would they tell me I was too gay? Would I be made to wear a uniform? Fuck, where would I buy a uniform that would *fit*?

At Charles Keene, Deane McQueen ran Performing Arts. She was a choreographer, performer, performing-arts specialist and was soon to be a major character in my life. Deane looked like no one else I had ever met. She dressed in androgynous sweats and multiple layers, and her hair was salt and pepper, cut short round the sides and spiked on top. She always wore lots of make-up with carefully crafted black eyeliner and taupe shadow. She was graceful and full of energy, often bois-terous and demanding; she was warm, domineering and she had a sometimes overpowering faith in all of her students – she truly believed all her pupils had what it took to make it in the business.

I went to meet Deane for the first time afraid, and totally lacking in self-confidence. I stood in front of her desk and told her how I'd been kicked out of school with no qualifications and how, after numerous dead-end jobs, I'd come to pursue my dream of being an actor. I couldn't look her in the eye and I kept my head bowed, too ashamed of myself and my dreams to hold my head up. My anxiety and worry almost overcame me, and if I could have gathered up the nerve, I would have turned round and left.

But the simple truth was that I had nowhere else to go. I had failed at almost everything in my life and I was paranoid I would never be able to break the trend. Not only did I have no clue who I was, I had no idea what I could be. I had been told for years I was stupid, ugly and disgusting and even when I had reinvented myself, I'd felt I had to play a character to get by. That loud and obnoxious persona had made me fail at school and the friends I had entertained like a class jester were no longer around to applaud. I felt worthless. Applying to Charles Keene was my cry for help.

Deane listened and then told me the course she thought would suit me best was the BTEC First Diploma in Performing Arts, led by a sensitive and brilliant ex-ballerina, Liz Valentine. It was a year-long course combining acting, dance and music with more theoretical areas of theatre, like stage management and arts management. As she explained it, I grew more and more aghast. The course seemed so big, enormous in fact. How could I, the fat, stupid kid, possibly learn all of those subjects in just one year? Acting was one thing, but arts management *and* dancing!

But even though I was scared, something felt different. The fear inside me was thrilling. Somehow, I already trusted Deane. Even then, in that first interview, she treated me differently, as no one ever had. It was as if she sensed that I had more to offer than just serving tables or selling double glazing. She listened to what I had to say and the more honest I was, the more she welcomed me into her world. I wasn't embarrassed to admit I was scared and I needed her to know I had fucked up at school. She could see my desperation and instead of laughing or rejecting me, she just listened and seemed to understand.

As I left her office, I was overcome by feelings of relief. I sat outside the dance studio and wept.

Even so, by the time I got home, I was certain I had failed once again. Why would Deane give a place to a timid, fat Chinese boy who had messed up so badly? I'd become accustomed to knock-backs and things not working out, and this didn't feel any different.

What I didn't know was that Deane had decided straight away that she was going to offer me a place. A few days later, to my astonishment and delight, I received my acceptance letter in the post. Mum and Dad were thrilled for me. I was officially going to college! My nerves were a mixture of fear and excitement but I also felt mature and optimistic. After all, I had achieved something, if only winning a place on a BTEC First course.

I started when I had just turned seventeen, in September 1992. Our days were spent proving why we had won our places on the course. We acted, danced, performed music, stage-managed and took theory classes. Within a couple of days I knew this was the right course for me as I thrived on the information I was being given. It felt amazing to be learning and I soaked up all they had to teach me like a sponge. The days were long and it took me several weeks to adjust to having a routine again, but it felt good to have somewhere to go each day.

The college was nothing like school. We were allowed to smoke in the refectory, our time management was our own responsibility and the others on my course had a whole variety of talents and aptitudes. Some were dancers with dreams of performing with Ballet Rambert; some were directors, technicians or managers who would later go on to work at Leicester's Haymarket Theatre; some were musically gifted and could play almost any instrument; and others, like me, were actors.

The Really Wild West Show was a thing of my past. The preacher and Dandini were no longer required as I was on to bigger and better things. I triumphed in my acting classes as I read Pinter, Chekhov, Orton and Osborne. My mind was exploding with information, and it was all stuff I was interested in. I improvised, cried, laughed and thought harder than I ever had before. I began to take control of my speech and the language I used, and it was as if I began to breathe properly for the first time. I watched the other students dissect scripts and I marvelled at how we were all interesting and unique, each of us with a valid opinion on a text. And I began to trust the people round me and make friends.

Even the dance classes were bearable, even enjoyable. My body was starting to move in different ways; I was no longer plodding my weight round with discomfort, making excuses for just living: I was suddenly aware of my space. I knew I was never going to be the next Nureyev but that was fine. I would bounce round the dance studio, hopping, stag-leaping, forward rolling – and I even once attempted a whole backwards roll! For the first time it didn't matter that I was fatter than all the other kids; in fact, in some ways it was an advantage. I could use all of my physical presence to demand attention on stage. No one was going to miss the overweight Chinese boy – he had arrived and he wasn't going anywhere!

The irony was that the more I performed and bounced about in my dance classes, the more weight I lost. It wasn't a considerable amount but it was enough to justify a double sausage sandwich each and every lunchtime. My peers didn't call me names, they never poked, prodded or pinched – they liked me. And I knew that, for the first time in my life, it wasn't because of the character I was portraying.

It was the real me.

The more my confidence soared, the happier I became. I was still working for Mum and Dad at the weekends but I was fulfilled because the restaurant wasn't my only focus. I knew it was a stop-gap while I trained as the country's next rising star. I had forgotten about the bullying, I was no longer a failure and I was even beginning to accept that being gay was a part of who I was.

I came to the scary decision that I would tell Oilen the truth about my sexuality, as she was the one I felt I could confide in. Oilen was at university by then, living in a flat with some girlfriends in Hendon, so I made the trip to go and see her. I was wearing a black-and-red tartan waistcoat, which is indelibly associated in my memory with the big moment.

I don't know what I was expecting, but I'd built up the whole thing my mind to the point where I was virtually expecting fireworks to go off and the bunting to come out when I made my big announcement.

I sat Oilen down and, with pounding heart and sweating hands, I looked at her and said, 'I think I'm gay.'

'I know that already,' was her distinctly unimpressed response. She said that she'd always suspected, right from the Gok-arina days, and it was no surprise at all. Later she said that her main feeling was one of worry; she knew that extra struggles and difficulties would lie ahead because of it.

My revelation may have been an anticlimax but it was still a relief to have someone who knew, and Oilen became my confidante. Not long afterwards, I told Kwok-Lyn, too, and it helped me that neither my brother nor my sister changed towards me one bit. I just wasn't sure how to go about telling the outside word.

There were a couple of other gay guys on the performing arts courses, both terribly flamboyant and happy in their own skin. Andrew was tall, spotty and a creative genius. His indie-style clothes looked as if they needed a wash but he didn't care about cleanliness as he had bigger things on his mind, such as art installations and semiotics. Fergus was a dancer who would *jeté* around the dance studio, his dreadlocks flowing, as he interpreted despair and frustration. Rumour had it he was bisexual. It felt wonderful to be around people who had accepted their sexuality and the more I watched, the more I became excited about what being gay really meant.

I had hidden my sexuality for so long, it had become a habit to avoid all conversations about girls and sex. But college felt safe and I knew my fellow students would allow me to be gay without judgement or rejection.

I was ready to admit to my sexuality but I had no idea how I was going to go about it.

Of course, I had fallen in with a group of girls on my course and we would all hang out in the refectory smoking, discussing performances, gossiping and, of course, *they* would discuss boys. Whenever the topic arose, I would blush to boiling point with embarrassment, make a hasty excuse (usually a desperate need for another double sausage sandwich) and rush off. It was unbearably humiliating because most of the time they were testing me to see if I would just admit to being a great big nancy – they knew, and I knew they knew!

One particular day, we were all sitting round in our dance kit waiting for a class to start when one girl started talking about who she thought was the fittest lad on the BTEC First. At the merest hint of this conversation, I began to panic that I'd be asked outright what I thought but I also couldn't stop listening. Most of them agreed it was bisexual Fergus, but one girl said she quite liked Dylan, a tall, blond-haired Donovan fan. A moment of insanity came over me and instead of blushing and running off to the canteen hatch, I said, in a high-pitched voice, crackly with nervousness, 'I think Dylan, too, but he does need to clean his nails a bit more!'

Immediately, I wanted to clap my hands over my face and beg someone to beat me with a chair – what the fuck had I done? The conversation ground to a halt and a horrendous, nervous silence swamped our group. I could feel myself flush but, to my surprise, it wasn't with embarrassment – it was with excitement. I stared at the floor for what felt like a day until one of the girls said, 'Dylan's okay but he thinks he's a fucking hippie, even though his mum and dad live in a massive house. And I know they're born-again Christians who vote Tory!'

At which point we all fell about in hysterics until we were called into class.

At last, I had finally come out. It wasn't terrible, no one had died and I hadn't lost any friends. All those years of panic, frustration and secrets dissolved in one nanosecond. I felt liberated. From that moment on I didn't feel guilty if I noticed a good-looking boy, I could join in with *all* the conversations with the girls and I was one step closer to being a happier me.

I was seventeen, fat and officially newly fabulous!

CHAPTER EIGHT

Isolation

The months rolled by and soon I was approaching the end of my course. I was predicted straight As – not bad for a beauty-school dropout – and Deane had asked me to enrol on the two-year BTEC National, the next course up.

I couldn't believe I was doing so well and, combined with coming out to my college friends, it meant my confidence rocketed. I decided I would complete the National course and then apply to a drama school in London – another step closer to my burning ambition of becoming an actor.

This was something I could never have contemplated doing twelve months before, when I'd arrived at college feeling completely beaten, but now I had the strength to consider putting myself forward for something like drama school. It was such a buzz to know I was good at something and that it happened to come with the potential of glamour and fortune. I would imagine myself living in a grand penthouse on Park Lane, eating in fine restaurants in London's West End and surrounding myself with interesting artists.

I couldn't wait to get away from home. I was bored with Leicester, and it would always remind me of those miserable days at school. I yearned to escape to where I could be someone else. I would see Big Ben on the ten o'clock news and become so excited, dreaming about the day when I would belong to the magical world that London had to offer.

London was, of course, the place I dreamed of going. I knew it was the capital of opportunity where everything was possible. It was where famous actors lived, read their scripts and practised their lines, all the time laughing, chatting and just being fabulous. London was where actors would find love and happiness because it was where their creativity was understood. People were attracted to actors and this meant people would be attracted to me, because I was going to be an ACTOR, darling! Just you wait, Henry Higgins, just you wait …

It was thoughts like these that dominated my mind and pushed me hard to succeed at college. My dream had begun and I was certain that if I worked hard enough, I could make sure it came true.

The last term had nearly ended and our coursework had been handed in. The girls and I decided to head into town for a drink to celebrate. We had had a dance lesson that morning so we were all dressed in our dance kit as we chatted and strolled into the town centre. I was wearing a red polo shirt, blue tracksuit bottoms and red Reebok Classic trainers – the outfit that would take me into the next stage of my life.

Town was busy that day, perhaps because giros had been issued, and people hurried through the streets or waited at bus stops laden with shopping, while jobless kids sauntered about or commandeered the benches. We were heading to a pub we knew well as it served *anyone*, as a few in our group were still seventeen.

As we walked to the pub, laughing and joking, we passed the Sainsbury's on Gallowtree Gate. It was one of the busiest parts of town then and as we approached the huge orange sign I felt a little strange and uneasy.

Ten yards in front of us stood a gang of boys, the oldest about twenty-one. There must have been eight of them, all dressed in their uniform of white trainers and oversized hoodies. The gang stared at me as I walked towards them and my instinct began to tell me that something wasn't right. The girls were oblivious and they walked on without taking much notice, still laughing and chatting. I, on the other hand, was gripped by terror, but it was too late to stop and turn back. I could only keep going, although I was now at the rear of our pack and almost on my own. My heart began to race and a feeling of sickness filled my throat and stomach. The gang must have seen the fear on my face as they grouped and bowled towards me, sinister grins on their faces. Blood rushed to my head as I panicked but I couldn't say anything or alert the girls, who were still walking on. They were round me in seconds, and the oldest leaped forward so that his face was almost touching mine. My entire body froze with fright. His face was inches away from mine and his body almost pressed against me – pushing me, edging me, intimidating me. I saw hate in his eyes and his mouth was a sight I would never forget: tight lips over yellow-stained teeth. His Afro was twisted into small dreadlocks and his breath reeked of drugs and cigarettes.

I wanted to turn and run but I couldn't. My helpless fat body was paralysed. The boy's chest jerked and he pushed me back, beating his chest with his hands as he did so, saying, 'What the fuck? Fucking batty boy! So ya think ya a big man, eh? Come! Wha gwan ya FUCKING QUEER!' As he said this, he began to smirk. He knew he had full control of every part of me. My face was burning hot and my mouth felt like it had never tasted water. My eyes began to fill with tears and my lips began to quiver with fear. His arms lashed out and he pushed me back again. I stumbled but I managed to regain my balance, not once letting go of his stare. He took a single step towards me until his nose was touching my cheek and he snarled, 'If I ever see ya dirty queer face in town again … I will fucking KILL you. Ya get me?'

I said nothing.

'I asked you a fucking question, batty boy, answer me!' he shouted but I couldn't speak. My jaw hung from my face like the joint had been disconnected. My mind was blank as my heart raced so fast I thought it might leap from my body. Frustrated and even angrier, he put his hand in the pocket of his tracksuit top and took hold of a knife-shaped object. Waving it around in his pocket and slowly walking backwards, he gave me one last snarl and said, 'Fucking bent queer ... I will KILL you.'

As the gang walked away spitting, laughing and congratulating one another, I stood in total isolation. Memories of being hated and bullied came rushing back. I felt helpless and terrified. I didn't want this to be happening. What had I done so wrong? Why did he want to kill me? Did the gang know something that I didn't? The shock of what had just happened hit me and a single humiliated tear fell as my body shook. I felt used, battered, broken and worthless. I felt like I was thirteen again but this was beyond the poking and pinching in school, this was something that you watched on the news or saw in movies. And it had just happened to me.

My friends had missed the whole incident but when I found them and told them, they couldn't believe they hadn't seen. They could tell I had been traumatised as I was white as a sheet. They hugged me with a combination of shock and guilt. The panic was over but I felt desperately unsafe and all I wanted was to be out of town and at home.

I called my brother and within minutes he was racing into town to collect me. I shall never forget what Kwok-Lyn did for me that day – it was a moment when I realised how much he meant to me, and how deeply he cared about me in return. Over the years we had grown apart, as many siblings do with the introduction of school and friends in our lives. In his teens Kwok-Lyn had become quiet and shy, and he didn't enjoy social events very much but just seemed happy to be on his own. He didn't enjoy the limelight of the front of house in the restaurant, he was far happier to be in the kitchen, hidden from the public. At school he kept a low profile, surrounding himself with the underdogs – the kind of kids you seem to forget the moment you leave them. Like Oilen and me, he had been a victim of bullying but it seemed to affect Kwok-Lyn differently. The name-calling and cruel words seemed to rebound off him, where the teasing would bury itself in my flesh and cause awful pain.

I will never forget the feeling of security I had when Kwok-Lyn arrived in town to collect me. I was safe again. With his chest puffed out to maximum stretch, he demanded to know who the boys were and what they had said and done. As I told him, I began to feel strong again because I knew he would never let anyone harm me. Then I became angry. I hated the gang. How dare they frighten me? I wanted them to die. I told Kwok-Lyn what they looked like and that the leader had threatened to kill me. I told him about everything except the knife-shaped object in the boy's pocket. I didn't tell because I was afraid this would impel my brother to hunt them down and he, too, would be threatened and maybe even stabbed. It was safer he only knew part of the story. We drove home in silence but when we got home I broke down and told Mum everything, even about the knife-shaped object, finding comfort from her shock and worry.

After that, my existence became a constant struggle of paranoia. I didn't go into town for fear that I might bump into the gang or their leader, nor would I go to the local shops or park in case they were there. The fear grew inside me and began to take over my life.

Even today, I am angry when I think about that boy – he really was no more than a boy – and the devastating effect he had on my life. I'm sure that he walked away from our encounter and got on with the rest of his life. I'm sure that what he said and did to me meant nothing to him; it was probably no more than a joke with his friends to kill time, and he most likely forgot about it almost immediately. He would have had no idea that he had just destroyed every ounce of the confidence I had fought so hard to get, and that he left me scared for the rest of my life.

As my paranoia grew, I decided that it wasn't only town that was off-limits but that I wasn't safe anywhere at all. I stopped going out of the house unless there was absolutely no other choice. A walk to the local shop became a mission I could only undertake after convincing myself that I would be okay. I had to really persuade myself to go anywhere or do anything, and when I did go out, I was haunted by fear. I began to obsess over it constantly. Life became like some kind of terrible minefield where the wrong step might bring instant oblivion. I convinced myself that certain places were safe and others were not – college classrooms were okay but the corridors were not. The small refectory was okay but the big one wasn't. The list went on. I taught myself to analyse my surroundings like a security expert, and I planned my routes as though I was under constant threat of assassination. I was constantly aware of exactly who was around me, even if they were barely in vision. The occasional visit to the pub became a military operation. I would case the bar, SAS-style, and if I felt uncomfortable or suspected any danger I would leave immediately. Before long I wasn't just afraid of the boy who had threatened me; everyone had become a potential threat.

I kept my fears to myself because I was sure it would sound ridiculous to others, so it became another secret that I coped with alone. In order to get through it, I focused everything on college and my dream of moving to London and going to drama school. It was now more than just a way of fulfilling my ambitions of being an actor. Moving to London was going to get me away from Leicester, get me away from my constant fear of the boy, the gang and anyone who might want to hurt me. London would be different – the city where the streets were paved with gold. I was more certain than ever that I simply had to get there for all my dreams to start coming true.

Ameneh's Easy Tom Yum Soup

INGREDIENTS

4 shallots, finely sliced
Thai green curry paste
Fish sauce
Galangal
Lemongrass
Sugar
Vegetable stock
Lime juice
Pak choi
Noodles

METHOD

Add the shallots, curry paste, fish sauce, galangal, lemongrass and sugar to the stock, bring to the boil and simmer. Chop in pak choi, add the noodles and a generous splash of lime juice. Simmer a little more and serve. Relaxed, sweet, spicy. Nourishing for the soul, great for clearing the head. Made with love xxx

Recipe by: Ameneh, the Human Pinball

CHAPTER NINE

Donovan versus Chapman

During my first term on the BTEC National, I began to find my stride again. I tried very hard to put the incident with the gang behind me and focus my attention on getting good grades. I immersed myself in my course, finding confidence in working hard, but always with a backwards glance over one shoulder.

I loved the acting lessons the most. I had a great lecturer named Kim Jackson. He was funny and flirtatious and made me feel good about myself. He treated me like an adult and I knew he valued what I brought to the lessons. I found that I could get lost in the acting classes; they allowed me to feel and think like a different person. While I was acting or studying a character, I could forget who I was and escape from the less-than-perfect reality.

The more I filled my mind with new information, the less space there was to think about how I was feeling about myself.

In some ways, I went back to being the person I was before my reinvention at school. Studying hard was my primary goal and keeping out of the way of people I didn't trust became an everyday activity. I did make some new friends on my course, though, and while I was studying and being creative I gave myself license to let go a little and try out my true personality. I took my first steps towards being the confident, outgoing and – all right – sometimes overbearing person I am today.

As my first year progressed, I felt that I wanted my own space so I decided that I would leave home. A few people on my course had already moved out and they'd told me that as I was in full-time education I would qualify for housing benefit. If I had housing benefit and worked for Mum and Dad at the weekends, I realised I could just about afford to find a place. I knew this was something I had to do if I was to ever find a boyfriend and fall in love.

One of Dad's customers was a small-time Leicester property mogul who owned a terraced house five minutes away from the restaurant, and I ended up going to look at it. The house was rundown and old, and had been turned into two small flats with a bedsit in the attic, but as we opened the front door, kicked away the mountains of post and climbed the three flights of stairs to the top, I started to feel excited and free.

The attic bedsit was hardly the lap of luxury and had the chalky smell of damp and mould. It was tiny, so small it wasn't even a bedsit – more of a bed*stand*. The carpet was deep grey and covered in stains, and the small window was made of slatted sheets of glass that stayed permanently open owing to a broken lever. The kitchen was no more than a sink and a draining board with a small trestle table next to it that held a one-ring electric stove. The shower was covered in mould where the seals had not been replaced in years and the toilet looked as if it was the main route for all the sewage in Leicester ... but I loved it at once. This was where I was going to find my independence and become the person I had wanted to be for so long.

'I'll take it!' I cried. The deal was done. For £30 per week including bills, this was going to be my new home. A trip to IKEA, a lick of yellow and blue paint and an old bedspread from Mum turned the hovel into my home, and I moved in, thrilled to have taken this important step.

The winter was painful, however. Because of my broken window, the freezing air would race into the attic and I would often find icicles on the ledge below, inside the room. Mum gave me a blow heater that just about stopped my breath from coming out in clouds of steam but it wasn't strong enough to thaw the sheet of ice that covered the shower-room walls.

Cold, mouldy and small – but all mine! Now the scene was set for me to fall in love.

Dylan, the hippie with dirty nails, was in his second year of the BTEC National and I'd already decided I liked him. He had long, blond hair and he wore corduroy flairs every day of the year. His wrists were decorated in so many friendship bracelets, he appeared to be the most popular person in the world, and my friend's suspicions about his Christian upbringing were correct.

I made no secret of my infatuation with Dylan and everyone seemed to know about it – maybe because he had played such a key role in my coming-out story. I would watch him leaping around the dance studio, my breath caught in my throat, and afterwards I would see him entertaining his fellow students in the refectory, discussing his love for the seventies and Donovan. I can still hear his singing floating through the refectory and into my heart.

My passion for Dylan grew and it wasn't long before I was reinventing myself again, this time encompassing the seventies' look of waistcoats, beads, friendship bracelets and flares. I was still overweight and looked more like a butch dyke than I did a hippie, but my heart told me that if I was to get Dylan to fall hopelessly in love with me, then I would need to appeal to his taste. My CD collection began to fill up with Simon and Garfunkel, Tracy Chapman and, of course, Donovan. My nights were filled with dreams of Dylan singing to me on his battered old guitar, serenading me as I fell asleep on his thick locks of gold. If the reality was that I was shivering under six blankets in my damp bedsit, well, at least my dreams were warm and cosy.

Then, to my surprise, Dylan began to notice me, and unless I was lost in a delusional world of arrogance, I could have sworn he was flirting! It was the signal I'd been dreaming of, and instantly I was completely taken over by my lust for him. He was all that I wanted, he was effortlessly cool and beautiful ... everything I wasn't, in fact. After several weeks of casual refectory liaisons, I plucked up enough courage to invite him to my flat for a beer and to listen to some records. To my complete delight and surprise, he accepted.

It was the longest wait of my life as I sat on my bed with Donovan blaring from my stereo. Had I said 8 p.m. or 9 p.m.? I watched the small travel clock next to my bed as the hands went slowly round: 7 p.m. to 7.03 p.m. to 7.08 p.m. After every track, I changed the music, desperately trying to decide which song would be best to welcome Dylan into my home. Tea lights flickered on every available surface; it was like sitting in a séance. 7.34 p.m. to 7.49 p.m. to 8.01 p.m.

The small broken window was at such a position that if I wanted to see into the street below, I had to balance one leg on the corner of my bedside table and hoist my fat and heavy body over the ledge to see anything other than my guttering. I couldn't sustain the position for very long before my weight pulled me back down on to the bed with a thump. But as the travel clock ticked on, I would hoist and slump, hoist and slump, hoist and slump in search of my beautiful boy, Dylan. The cheap tea lights were burning quickly and I was soon scurrying about trying to replace them as they guttered out one by one. My stocks were running low and I knew I MUST have a flat full of delicate lighting for when Dylan arrived, but I couldn't blow them out because if I missed the sound of his car and he surprised me with his arrival then I wouldn't have enough time to light them all, and my choreographed welcome would be ruined! Hoist and slump, light candles, hoist and slump, re-light candles, hoist and slump, light more candles ... 8.24 p.m. to 8.41 p.m. to ... 9 p.m.!

The hollow feeling of rejection began to grow as the hands of the bastard travel clock ticked by. Fortunately, mobile phones were a luxury in those days otherwise I am quite certain there would have been numerous anonymous calls to find out where he was. Was he sick? Had he had a car crash? Was he not coming? I feared the worst and at 9.30 p.m. I decided that Dylan was either dead or he had absolutely no interest in the fat Chinese kid. I blew out the tea lights, switched off the music and lay down on my bed, heartbroken and filled with disappointment. I closed my eyes, trying to not cry over him as he *wasn't* worth my tears ... But I couldn't help it, and I sobbed into my pillow.

BUZZZZ!!!!!!!

I had fallen asleep in my sadness and the sound of my doorbell woke me. It was 10.01 p.m. and Dylan had arrived. I rolled off my bed, grabbed the box of kitchen matches from the table and rushed about frantically, lighting all thirty tea lights, burning my fingers as I went. The buzzer was going crazy as I fluffed the pillows, set Donovan to sing again and re-arranged the ninety sets of beads round my neck. You have never have seen a fat person move more quickly as I bolted down the three flights of stairs, avoiding the post, rubbish and flaking wallpaper as I went.

I stood at the closed door, heart racing and sweat pouring past my swollen eyes. Dylan was on the other side of my front door and I couldn't have been happier. I hastily gathered myself and opened the door coolly. As I saw his beautiful smile and his long, thick, blond hair, it didn't matter that his nails were probably dirty – he was a vision of perfection!

We went upstairs and as we went into the bedsit, he remarked how much he loved candlelight. YES! Get in there!

The late evening was filled with endless chat about music – most of the artists I'd never heard of but pretended I had. Dylan made me feel attractive, confident and like there was no place he would rather be. I noticed how in the candlelight his eyes looked almost Chinese as the sides pulled away from his face in neat little points. His lips were perfect curves and slightly pinked by the hot tea. His neck was long and his strong dancer's shoulders were just visible under his home-knitted jumper. I was experiencing my first real sexual crush and it felt divine.

We didn't kiss or touch that night, let alone have sex. I didn't even know if Dylan was gay. It didn't matter. In my heart, he was mine. I was hopelessly in love with him and even if he wasn't gay, I was prepared to convince him otherwise. The confidence I had found at college enabled me to think like this. I was, after all, one of the stronger performers in my year and Dylan knew that, so surely that was enough to seduce him? I had certainly changed over the last year – I was developing into a young adult and I welcomed it with fat, open arms. I didn't want to be the bullied kid any more, I didn't want to be the stupid brother or the panicked scared gay boy; I wanted to be a man who could love and contribute to an adult relation-ship, and Dylan was going to help me. In return, I would be loyal and love him until the day we died.

We reached the early hours of the morning, pissed and exhausted. Dylan said it was time for him to leave as he was up early in the morning. Fuck me! There was no way I was going anywhere till gone lunch.

We said our goodbyes and Dylan left my bedsit. As I flopped ecstatically on my bed, I did consider hoisting myself over the window ledge to see him drive away but I knew it would have been like hauling the *Titanic* out of the ocean, so I lay, happy, fulfilled and very, very drunk, until I drifted into the best night's sleep of my life.

The next few days at college were strange. I couldn't concentrate on my lessons and all I could think about was Dylan. He had taken over my consciousness and become the most important person in my life. I was even too scared to tell the girls in case they told me that I was wasting my time, or laughed at my infatuation.

Love was a new emotion in my life and I wasn't sure how to deal with it. Dylan, though, was just the same towards me as he had been before his visit. He was still leaping round the dance studio and singing in the refectory ... In fact, everything was the same. It was as if he had never come over that night, drunk my beer and listened to my music. Why wasn't it different? Why wasn't he blushing when he spoke to me? Why were there no butterflies in his tummy when he saw me? Why was he not in love with me like I was with him?

Going out of my mind with confusion, I asked him if he wanted to come over again. To my absolute shock, he agreed. Now I got it! He was gay but he was still dealing with coming out. If he had been overly friendly with me at college, it would have blown his cover so he was just playing it cool. Oh, Dylan. You beautiful, confused and innocent soul!

That night, the candles were lit, the fridge was stocked with beer and Donovan once again filled the bedsit. This was going to be the night we would confess our love for one another and, perhaps, Dylan might even stay over ...

That night I waited and waited ... and waited. Dylan didn't arrive, he didn't drink my beer and he didn't serenade me on his guitar. I guess his no-show was his way of letting me know he was just not interested.

Strangely, I dealt with his rejection better than I could have dreamed of. I didn't hate him, I didn't feel awkward when I saw him at college and I didn't invite him over again – because I couldn't blame him. Why would someone so very beautiful be attracted to someone like me – fat, scared and inexperienced? I wasn't good enough for him and probably never would be. How could I have been so stupid as to believe that my abilities in the drama studio were enough to make someone fall in love with me?

CHAPTER TEN

London's Calling

Deane McQueen had made it very clear that she was expecting big things from me, and a top drama school was part of her master plan. I suppose I had become her personal project. She had dragged me from the gutter and turned me into a straight-A student with as much opportunity as any of her pupils. I felt I owed it to her to at least apply, maybe I would even get a place.

The first time I heard of Central was when I looked through the UCAS handbook and saw that The Central School of Speech and Drama was advertising some courses that were funded by the government.

My dream was to study straight acting but the problem was that performance courses were not government funded so the fees – often hefty – had to be paid for privately. It was a big obstacle for me as there was no way my parents could afford that kind of money, even if it would make my dreams come true. Mum and Dad's business was barely making enough money to keep noodles on the table, let alone send their son to London, pay for his rent and living costs as well as the course fees.

Much to many budding performance artists' excitement, Central had just started offering part-academic, part-performance courses in Drama and Education, and Speech Therapy, designed for people who wanted a career in teaching rather than on the stage.

It didn't mean anything to me because I had no idea what The Central School of Speech and Drama was. I didn't have a clue that it was one of the most prestigious drama schools in the country, sitting alongside the famous RADA in the nation's affections, or that its prestigious alumni included many of my heroes, including Dawn French and Jennifer Saunders, to name but two. But I could see that it was something special from the way Deane regarded it with awe and UCAS made it appear so grand and exclusive. There were artistic, black-and-white photos of students performing in great spaces in full costume, dancing in mirrored studios or relaxing on the campus.

I could see that Central was a big thing for actors, and no one else on my course was considering applying for such a place. I considered myself the best performer in my year and my confidence was the highest it had ever been. I knew I was good at what I was doing and, what was more, my mindset had changed over the last year. I'd begun to develop a hard, competitive edge. I focused entirely on my ambition to be an actor and I was desperate to get a place at drama school and get out of Leicester as a big 'fuck you' to everyone who had told me I was useless and a failure. I turned their taunts to my advantage, to give me the courage to do what I could never have dreamed of doing a year ago.

As I read through the prospectus, I figured the Drama and Education course was my best option. Not only was it government funded but it had the most performance-based lessons, and learning to be a teacher would be an added bonus: when Spielberg or the National Theatre didn't require me, I would need to fill the gaps somehow – and not with teaching? It was bound to beat packing prawn crackers!

My goal was to get accepted, and thereby make Deane's dream come true – my gift to her for believing in me. Then I would move to magical London and wow them all at Central. The lecturers would spot my amazing potential, be overwhelmed by my talent and ask me to switch, and I would begin my second year on the straight acting course. The rest was easy: graduate, find an agent, begin work at the RSC and marry Simon Callow – how simple!

Gazing at the pictures in the UCAS handbook, I imagined how next year the school would ask if I would mind having my photograph taken for the prospectus. Why wouldn't they? They were definitely missing a young, fat, Chinese boy.

I applied and, to my delight, I was asked to attend an interview and audition. Once I realised it was actually going to happen, the enormity of how important this next stage was crept up and bit my big yellow ass: I was petrified.

Deane, however, was overjoyed. Her protégé was about to audition at London's Central School of Speech and Drama and she was over the moon.

The big day arrived and up I went to London, shaking in my shoes but knowing I had to go through with it. I had done my research since applying and I now understood what Central meant. This was a big deal.

The day itself knocked a lot of my dreams out of me. For one thing, Central is in Swiss Cottage, which is hardly the most glamorous part of London. When I arrived, I was puzzled: where was the Thames? Where was Big Ben? Was this actually London? It looked like a bit of a dump, with its shabby shops and down-at-heel pub on the middle of a roundabout.

At Central I had to do an improvisation class, which I felt fine about as that was my biggest strength at college, and have an interview. I was relieved that I didn't have to sing, as I was sure I was a rubbish singer (my memory of being downgraded to triangle basher at school had buried itself deep in my subconscious). I was nervous but both parts went all right – as far as I could tell, I didn't fuck up.

Afterwards I sat on the steps of the amphitheatre thinking I'd bitten off a lot more than I could chew – and for a twenty-one-stone overeater, that was saying something. The kids round me were from all over the country and they seemed to come from other worlds of money, privilege and education. They all seemed to be slim and attractive and, fuck me, were they clever! They spoke like grown-ups, in beautifully modulated voices, using long and fancy words with careless abandon. The girls flicked their hair a lot and the boys all seemed very serious as they name-dropped classical writers, drama practitioners, theorists and methods I'd never heard of.

I felt so different from them all and I was hurt that they took absolutely no notice of me. They'd seen me – you could hardly miss me and I stood out there even more than usual – but none of them made the effort to say hi, except for a couple of the shyer girls. I wanted to tell them all that I was the best actor in my year, and that I was going to be the country's next big star, but no one seemed in the least interested, so I kept my nervous mouth shut.

By mid-morning, I knew I had spent the last three years on courses that had not prepared me for drama school. My BTECs had taught me how to jump round a studio interpreting pain and anger, or to lie on the floor and pretend to be a fried egg, but it had not taught me the Stanislavski method. Deane was very enthusiastic about contemporary dance, so I had learned the importance of DV8, Candoco and V-tol on the performance circuit, and I had learned I had a natural ability to improvise, but what was that compared to the superior skills and solid learning of the people I was competing against?

I felt more stupid that day than I have ever felt in my entire life.

At the end of the day, as I walked down the steps and away from Central, I hoped that I would not get in. Surely the interviewers would realise I was not right for the course, class or school. As far as I was concerned, that was probably the last I would have to do with The Central School of Speech and Drama. Downhearted and feeling as thick as my waistline, I got on my coach at Victoria Station and headed back to Leicester, after having bought the entire contents of McDonald's for my journey home. My ambition to tread the boards had not entirely been shattered, surely there was a drama school out there for me where I would fit in?

Back in Leicester, I returned to the house I was sharing with a classmate, Sarah. After a year in my bedsit, I'd become a bit lonely all on my own, so Sarah and I had found a place to share in Aylestone. I had decorated my bedroom in newspapers – I was trying to be avant garde, I think, but it probably just looked ridiculous.

Me and Mum when I was about one year old, sat in our first home – the caravan

The last photo of me as a slim child, aged 3 or 4, outside my grandad's restaurant, The Hung Lau

Mum and Dad
in Abbey Park,
Leicester, 1969

Mum and Dad's
wedding day,
1970

Mum and me in
Portsmouth in 1976

Kwok-Lyn, Nan and
me on the ferry
going to the Isle of
Wight in 1977

From left to right: Kwok-Lyn, Oilen, Nan and me outside our shiny new council house in Beaumont Leys, 1979

Kwok-Lyn and me in The Bamboo House – How camp was I ???

Mum, Dad, Kwok-Lyn, Oilen and that's me in the middle, at The Bamboo House, 1980

Kwok-Lyn, Oilen, me and Mum on the Rally behind the estate with our dogs Lady and Podge, from around 1983

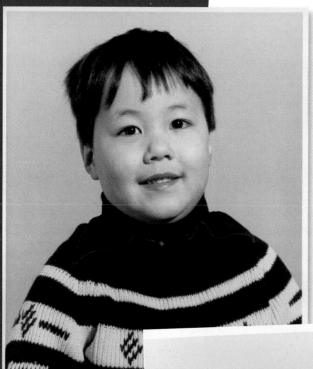

My first school pic, 1979

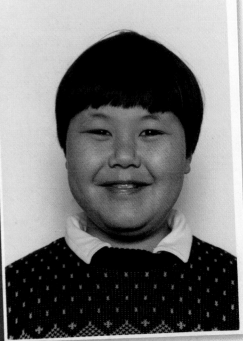

A growing boy, 1985

Aged 17

My new look after my
reinvention in 1987.
The kiss curl had been
replaced with a Bond-like
comb back – NICE!

In my third term at Central in 1996 – at this
point I still didn't think I was thin enough

A very talented dancer, Sarah had a shaved head, dozens of piercings and a Celtic tattoo wrapped around her upper right arm. We'd become close friends in our first year and, after she went through a turbulent break up with her boyfriend, we decided to find a place together.

Sarah was typical of many girls who come from loving, upper-working-class families. Before she had had her head shaved, she'd been an obedient girl with long, dark hair that was scrapped into a bun every Saturday for ballet class. She had studied hard and was told she was above standard for her age, so she had decided dance was going to be her life – well, except for drink and ZZ Top. As she got older, the docile student had grown angry, rebellious and determined to 'fuck the system', and she really went for it.

Sarah liked the fact I was fat, gay and mixed race – it appealed to her left-of-centre attitudes – and I quickly became a mascot for her anti-establishment campaign. She took me to Goth pubs, we went drinking in indie clubs and when we'd had way too much Jack Daniels, we would go back to our house and watch chick flicks in our PJs. It was a perfect combination of Alice Cooper meets *Alice in Wonderland*.

I loved Sarah. She was unlike anyone I had ever met, and she was liberating and exciting to be around. But she wasn't always the loud, angry rebel. Deep inside her Dr Martens, she was just as scared as I was, just as lonely and, at times, maybe even more confused than me. It was good to be back home.

A couple of weeks later, I received a letter from Central. To my absolute astonishment, I was being offered a place on the Drama and Education course, to start that autumn. I was so excited, I could hardly think straight, but I rushed to college immediately to tell Deane. She was sitting in her cubbyhole office by the dance studio, and I took a second to puff out my chest before I went in – I knew this was the best present I could possibly give her.

Deane was overjoyed – she screamed and hugged me, and then grabbed the letter from me and ran off to tell everyone, leaving me standing there. I didn't mind – this was what it had all been about after all. It was a big thank you to Deane for taking me under her wing and helping me when I'd been at my lowest. My mission was complete.

Except for one thing.

Now I actually had to go to London and take up my place on the course.

That summer I went down to London to look for accommodation – I found a miniscule bedsit in Kilburn, not too far from the campus. My whole focus was now on London and the life and opportunity that lay in front of me. I was finally on my way. My deeply cherished dream of becoming an actor was that much closer to coming true.

Of course I had my doubts and fears – in my heart, I

was sure that I wasn't going to match up to those golden-skinned, clever students I had seen at the auditions – but surely the school knew what it was doing by accepting me? If they had faith that I could do an academic course, then surely I should have faith in myself?

This was my chance to stick two strong and dramatic fingers up at the bullies and the gangs – all those who, over twenty years, had told me I was worthless, stupid, fat and no good. Well, FUCK THE LOT OF YA! London was calling me.

CHAPTER ELEVEN

Central

The Central School of Speech and Drama is one of the greatest drama schools in the world. It trains people not just how to be actors, but also how to be stage managers, speech therapists, set designers or even teachers. The school was once home to some of this country's greatest talents: Laurence Olivier, Judi Dench, Julie Christie, Christopher Eccleston, Kristin Scott Thomas and Rufus Sewell are just some of the famous alumni.

I arrived from Leicester with thirty quid in my back pocket and the determination and desperation to make it, just like everyone else arriving that autumn (acting institutions are like fly traps for dysfunctional kids who are all out to prove themselves, regardless of the consequences). Some people there were content to be teachers, therapists or theory practitioners but I was hungry for success and stardom, and I was willing to sell my soul to the school to get it.

When I arrived at Central, I was big: a twenty-one stone, larger-than-life force to be reckoned with. I had bleached-blond hair and a ring on every finger. I had developed a bravado that allowed me to face any situation and my ambition leaked out of every pore. I had been the queen of my last college and I was determined to remain royal.

I moved into the tiny studio flat that I had rented during the holidays. It was on the ground floor of a Georgian house on a leafy street that wouldn't have looked out of place in a prestigious area of Leicester. The house was beautiful and had, no doubt, once been a grand home before it had been converted into flats. Mine was even pokier than the one I'd had in Leicester. My one small room was just big enough for a single bed, a chest of drawers and a little wardrobe. At one end of the room was a door that led to the bathroom, so small there was barely enough room for its shower, sink and toilet. Across the hallway and under the stairs was my kitchen. It had just enough space for a two-ring Baby Belling stove sitting on top of a tiny cupboard next to an even smaller sink. The kitchen was so cramped, I couldn't stand up straight. The flat was cold, depressing and overpriced at £70 per week, but I didn't care. If everything went according to plan, then this was where I was going to become a famous actor, and humble beginnings were all part of the struggle on the path to success.

On the first day of enrolment new students were to meet in the main reception of the school at 10 a.m. When I arrived, I saw a mix of kids, all young except one or two mature students, all bright-eyed, hungry for knowledge and blinded by ambition. Like a pack of young wolves, we quickly set about sussing out the hierarchy: who was the loudest, who was the most confident, who was the leader and who were the followers? Right away I met a Brummy girl called Jessica – Jess for short – who was cute and friendly; a tall, glamorous, older girl called Emma; and Lydia, a short, Greek girl who later told me that her first impression of me that day was that I was loud, friendly, full of smiles and confident. Little did she know the six-foot, fat Chinese lad was scared shitless and struggling more than anyone.

I had taken one look at everyone else and instantly felt like I didn't fit in. My face was different, my mannerisms were different; even my language was different. Most of the group looked as if they could have been siblings; they all seemed to be very beautiful with perfect skin and tousled, trendy hair, and of course they were slim. All of this made me feel deeply insecure. Now, of course, I'm sure that they all came with their own insecurities and doubts, but to me then they seemed absolutely unafraid. I wondered how they could be so fearless. Had they been told what to expect? Perhaps they had received a handbook and mine had been lost in the post?

As I'd learned to do whenever I found myself in situations that were foreign to me, I began to speak louder, crack jokes aimed at myself and flit very quickly among the others, assessing them all and working out my role. I clearly wasn't the clever one, I definitely wasn't the pretty one and, without a shadow of a doubt, I wasn't the confident one. So I was the joker, making cheap gags for cheap rent. I was determined not to let my physical appearance be the focus of attention so I carefully created the false assumption that I didn't have a care in the world. I used my usual weapons – humour and self-deprecation – to draw attention away from my size. I'm sure that a trained observer would have seen exactly what I was doing and realised my bravado was all a front to hide my insecurities, but the other students seemed taken in.

The alter ego I created that day still lives with me. When I am interviewed on a chat show, thrust into conversation on a red carpet or when I've done something wrong and I need to diffuse the situation, I panic and my alter ego appears. This other Gok is self-confident and thrives on being noticed. He is suave, cultured, sophisticated and even – dare I say it – charismatic. He is never at a loss for words and always ready with a witty one-liner or a joke. The main thing is that he is never lost or lonely or afraid. I often wish he really was me, and I really were him, but I'm not and never will be. The insecure, isolated kid inside me who craves acceptance and approval never goes away. Anyone who has been in a situation similar to mine and survived it will probably know what I mean. That first day at Central, my alter ego was working overtime, pumping out the aura of self-belief and making sassy comments at any opportunity.

Once our group had congregated in the main reception, we were asked to go up one floor to the refectory where we would meet our tutor and have an opportunity to ask questions.

We were all sitting in the cafeteria when Helen McNally appeared. No one saw her arrive and her dramatic entrance was clearly part of her act to make maximum impact on the new students. With her hair in a careless topknot and a flowing scarf hanging loosely round her neck in artistic unkemptness, Helen looked unmistakeably creative. She glided through the group to take centre stage at the front of DE98 (BA Hons in Drama and Education – Graduation 1998).

Helen seemed nothing like Deane, who had loved to laugh and was warm, compassionate and encouraging. She didn't appear to have those qualities; she looked as though she meant business and she'd approach her job sternly and methodically. But, after all, this school was about getting us qualified and working, and Helen was clearly not going to let up until she'd achieved that goal.

Our group hushed to an uneasy silence. Helen began to call a register of students and we sat quietly waiting to hear our names called. Most of the other students responded to their names with a firm 'Yes' and a broad smile, or a quiet whisper, or a studiedly casual 'Yeah'. Unfortunately, I did none of the above. When Helen called my name, I jumped to my feet as though I was bursting with confidence and said in a camp voice, 'Helen, darling, don't bother calling me Gok Wan … Let's just keep it to Gok, like Cher or Madonna?' and then bounced back into my chair and awaited my acknowledgement from the group.

While everyone else laughed, it was clear that Helen was not impressed. She half-looked up from her clipboard and shot me a glare from over the top of her glasses, staring at me for what felt like an eternity. The group quickly composed themselves and Helen nodded slowly as if to say, 'You silly fuck, do you have any idea who you are messing with? I could eat you up and spit you out before you even realised what was happening!' But she said nothing and continued with the register, occasionally shooting me that same glare until all the names had been read.

All my bravado melted away at once, and I was gutted at my behaviour. What the hell had I been thinking? I had made an enemy of the one ally I needed if I had any chance of ever passing this course. What a stupid wanker!

The truth was that I was in entirely the wrong place. I should have been in the studio next door, enrolling with the actors, people like me – stupid, but good with a crowd! The Drama and Education course was not right for me at all. For one thing, I wasn't clever enough. My strengths weren't essays and teaching drama, they were raising gags, acting the fool and performing.

I had a feeling that my brash, confident alter ego was not going to be slick enough to get me out of this one.

My first term at Central was difficult. I missed my friends and family, and London seemed too big to understand. I felt lost in my new, busy world and it was only the phone calls home that kept my spirits up. Living by myself in my Kilburn studio flat didn't help my loneliness.

Things improved when I made some friends – there was a group of us, including Jessica, Lydia, Emma, Carrie and Will – but life at Central was very hard work. We were in school at 9 a.m. and only finished at 6 p.m. In the opening of the television series *Fame*, one of the teachers says that the school is where the students will start paying their dues 'in sweat', and that's exactly how it felt for us. We were expected to give everything we had to the classes at all times, and we all did.

Our course was a large one, with a lot of practical aspects as well as academic classes. We had to read and study texts, plays and theories of performance, and we had essay assignments. We looked at education, school practices and teaching practices, as well as having classes in costume, stage management and direction. We even had work placements outside Central. All in all, we were kept very busy.

It was strenuous and hard work, which was excellent training as it implanted in us all a good work ethic and we knew what would be required of us in the world outside if we wanted to get anywhere. We were all so busy it felt we hardly had time for our friendships, let alone relationships, and although I had the odd crush on other students, nothing was happening in that department, which reinforced my sense of isolation, despite my new friends.

Things were not helped by the fact that my relationship with Helen, my tutor, never really improved beyond that first day. I was too far removed from the kind of person she wanted on her course, which was the academic side of the school. I'm sure she felt I wasn't suited to it, and she was probably right. I had come from Deane's strong maternal protection and guidance, and was probably looking for more of the same from my new tutor, but I wasn't going to get it from Helen and we ended up having a turbulent relationship that did nothing to help my struggles to cope with the workload.

It wasn't just that there was so much to do; it was the fact that I wasn't trained for it. The first time I got my work back, I was told quite frankly that it was bad and that I couldn't write an essay – but no one had ever taught me how to write one, and it appeared that they weren't about to start now. As a result, I felt increasingly stupid.

If it hadn't been for the course, I would have had a wonderful time at Central. I enjoyed the company of my new friends, and there was plenty of fun to be had. I loved hanging out at the student union – in the evenings, it was usually packed with all the Central types drinking and socialising. The actors would be on the steps of the school, drinking Jack Daniels and Coke and being über cool; the stage managers would huddle in the corner avoiding all eye contact; and the drama ed students would scatter around the bar, trying desperately not to look nerdy. Life outside the work was great – I loved exploring the city and all its shops and markets, going out clubbing in London and just generally being a student. I had always loved the party scene and everything that came with it, but I was well aware my life had been, and probably would always be, full of addictions, so I remained cautious yet typically experimental. But it seemed that nothing could help me when it came to the workload.

As the weeks went by at Central, I found it ever harder to keep up with the other students. Everyone found the work challenging but no one more than me. The assignments were getting tougher and my grades had begun to reflect that I was struggling. I was called into Helen's office and informed that she was concerned about the standard of my work and she would be keeping an eye on my progress. Hearing her confirm my worst fears was terrible.

I knew in my heart I was not clever enough for the course but now there was nowhere to hide. I had been rumbled. In desperate moments, I considered leaving Central but it wasn't really an option. How could I return to Leicester a failure, after I had promised my friends and family I was going to be an actor with my name in bright lights? My parents had sacrificed what little spare money they had to help me survive in London and I felt duty-bound to return to Leicester in three years' time, armed with a degree and able to show that their money had been well spent. I also felt a huge amount of pressure not to disappoint Deane because she had been so excited about me getting on to the course. If I left, I would not only be letting myself down, I would also be letting down my old college, the place that had saved me from a world of no prospects. If I returned to Leicester without my degree, I was going to confirm everyone's suspicions and my own deepest fears: I was the stupid, fat boy who was just full of dreams and lies. Central was the only achievement I was proud of and I knew I was fucking it up.

And that's when I decided that if I was ever going to succeed at Central – and by extension, in life – then I would have to look like everyone else. It was time to stop being the fat kid. Only if I were slim would I ever have a chance of getting through this.

So the answer was simple. FUCK YOU, FOOD!

CHAPTER TWELVE

Starvation

As the end of the first term at Central approached, I stood outside the school with Lydia. She had become a great friend and confidante. I touched my chest with both hands and told her, 'I just want to be slim. I want to feel beautiful and I want to be popular.'

Lydia looked shocked. I'd convinced her, just as I had everyone else on my course, that I was happy in my skin. Lydia tried to comfort me and tell me that everyone liked me just as I was, but I didn't believe her.

It was now time to be honest. I had to come clean once and for all. I was tired and worn out with pretending everything was okay when, for so many years, it hadn't been. The truth was that I loathed my body. I was embarrassed by it, hating the way it moved differently from everyone else's. I felt strongly that my size stood between me and success, and I wanted to feel attractive, just once, so I could have the same opportunities as everybody else. I even blamed my body for stopping me from getting an education. If I'd not been such a fool to believe I could get ahead in life just by making people laugh and by being the outgoing, bubbly, fat kid, then maybe I would have stayed in school and I wouldn't be struggling now. I also blamed my body for never letting me find love. Who could possibly find this lumpy, fat mess attractive if I couldn't even bear to look at it? Everyone round me was so beautiful. They were all falling in love with each other and yet again I was left on the bench.

Even though I had come out, I was still coming to terms with being gay. I knew 'gay' was who I was but I hadn't experienced sharing my sexuality with a man I loved. How could I? What if he fell for my mind and soul but when I revealed this sagging mass of flesh, he turned and ran for the hills, repulsed by what he saw? It would hurt too much. The risk was too high. It was easier to pretend I was happy just as I was.

I convinced myself that if I looked like everyone else, then maybe I would have a better chance of getting through the course or, better still, of getting my break at being an actor. It seems ridiculous now, but I was completely muddled by the many emotions I was experiencing – doubt, guilt and fear of failure, to name just a few. I knew deep down that being slim would never make me more intelligent or better equipped to pass my course or even make me an actor, but a voice in my head was telling me that if I was going to fail the course, then I needed to succeed at something, simply to alleviate the guilt.

But another part of me was scared to be slim. What if I lost my personality? It was the one thing about me that people didn't find grotesque. It was the one thing that had got me into Central, my biggest and only achievement so far in life. But my fear was replaced with determination. I wanted to prove to everyone on my course I was not stupid and I had as much chance of being successful as any of them. So what if they were rich or beautiful? I was going to be thin; and the thinner I was, the more success- ful I'd be. By now my brain had been programmed to believe the only way I was going to achieve at Central was if I was as skinny as the models in the magazines and the students on my course. I began to diet but of course I had no idea about how to diet healthily. I'd never been educated about nutrition and I didn't understand the importance of healthy eating or even know what it was. So when it came to slimming, it didn't occur to me to lose weight any other way than by simply cutting out food. I would stop eating so much, and then I would become slim. That was how it worked, surely? Before I began my diet, I ate a gargantuan meal of a bag of pasta, a whole jar of mayonnaise and two cans of tuna. It was a lot of food, but I considered it healthy because it wasn't fried. Then I began to cut down. I continued to eat three meals a day but I avoided fried food and anything fatty and I reduced my portion sizes.

After a few weeks of insignificant results, I grew impatient. I was desperate to lose weight before returning to Leicester for the Christmas holiday, as this was when I planned to debut my new, slimline body. I thought it would be important to impress my family with my weight loss because then they wouldn't know I was failing at Central. I needed to achieve results and there was only one way to do this: I would cut down even further.

My food intake began to get smaller and the hunger pains in my belly increased. I'd never felt real hunger before and the sharpness of the pain surprised me. I tried to ignore it, but it was hard to think about anything else when my stomach was growling and aching and begging for the kind of food I usually filled it with. But I was determined not to give in to its demands.

I started to keep a food diary and every day I wrote in it what I had eaten and how many calories I had consumed that day. Each day I tried to eat a little less than I had the day before.

The diary became my new addiction. I still have it today. I have never found the courage to throw it away, maybe because it reminds me of how I never want to feel again or perhaps because it reminds me, in a sick way, of something I never failed at.

When I returned to Leicester for the Christmas holiday, my family noticed I'd lost a small amount of weight. I enjoyed the constant compliments of how well I looked, and the positive attention allowed me to forget how miserable I had become. I'd lost around a stone and it was very noticeable, but it wasn't long before the big family feasts and tins of chocolates and biscuits made me forget my diet and I regained most of the weight I'd lost.

It didn't matter because I was happy again. I was around my family and old friends, and I felt secure and loved. I didn't care about diets or food diaries because I had the people I loved round me. For a short time Central didn't matter and my loneliness disappeared. Instead, I told my family how well I was getting on in London, how I'd made some new friends who were interesting and creative, just like me. I regaled them with stories of drunken nights in the student union, of getting the Tube late at night and of just how amazing and perfect my world at Central was. It felt okay to lie because I thought I was protecting them. After all, if I told them the truth they would only worry about me and I would revert to that dependent idiot child I so wanted to forget.

On Christmas day, Mum handed me a small box and I unwrapped it to find a key inside.

'Look out of the window,' she said, smiling at my confused expression.

When I looked out, I saw a shiny green Beetle sitting in the car park below. Mum had tied a huge red ribbon round it. I was so grateful – what amazing parents I had! They were skint but had saved for months to be able to give me this present.

Outwardly, I seemed ecstatic, but deep down, however, I was wracked with guilt. They had such faith in me. I couldn't let them down. I was determined to return to London, not only with a new car but also a renewed agenda: I was going to be slim and that was going to make me successful.

The first few weeks back at school were tough. The New Year blues set in and I was soon missing home. The car had been shown off and had lost its novelty value, and I realised I'd gained weight again. My coursework was overdue and my low was getting lower.

I began to write in my food diary once again, cutting back on my meals and creating new rules for myself, restricting the foods I was allowed. Anything I thought was fattening was out and my intake began to shrink. I'd already cut out cakes, sweets, chocolates and crisps, and all the junk I'd once loved so much. Now I began to restrict my intake of meat, fish, bread, pasta and, of course, fats and sugars. I let myself have some cereals, jacket potatoes and rice, salads, fruit and yoghurt. It felt good to be back on track but this time, the diary alone wasn't fulfilling my need for control. It wasn't enough to know what I had eaten each day; I wanted to see results.

I needed to eat even less. Food was evil; I was beginning to understand that. It amazed me how much I had once stuffed into my mouth and I took pleasure in denying myself what I would once have gorged on. It was very satisfying to forbid myself foods and to restrict the portions that I allowed myself. But the weight loss was *still* too slow. I decided it would be better if I ate as little as I possibly could – just enough to function on. And I started to take laxatives.

A friend had told me that laxatives were a quick way to lose weight, as they caused the food to move through you before it could be absorbed and turned into fat. It sounded like a good idea, and I assumed that they must be harmless since they could be bought over the counter in every pharmacy. The first packet I ever bought was called Sure Lax. Each tablet was about the size of a 20-pence piece and tasted of raspberries. I read the instructions and began taking the recommended dosage. It was amazing. I would take a couple of tablets the night before, wake up in the morning, go to the toilet and clear out yesterday's food. What *control*. Not only could I continue eating small amounts, I could also guarantee the food wouldn't stay in me long enough to cause any weight gain.

It worked well for a while, and I saw my weight begin to drop off me. But my body quickly became immune to the recommended dosage, so I began increasing the amount of laxatives I was taking. Within two weeks, I was tripling my dosage to get my hit. And then the pains began. I remember the agony so very clearly. The laxatives were rotting my gut and I could feel the acid burning the lining of my stomach. I would often wake in the middle of the night bent over in pain, and the only way of stopping the agony was to punch myself in the tummy. It was like being kicked time and time again, and every part of me throbbed as my body screamed for food and protested against those 'harmless' little pills. But I was determined not to give in. I was losing weight but I wanted to lose more, and faster. I kept on taking the laxatives.

The sleepless nights and lack of energy started to take its toll on my already lacklustre coursework. I began missing lectures, doing just enough work to keep my tutors off my back, and my absence from the school was starting to alarm my fellow students. My friends were worried about me but they couldn't do much more than ask if I was all right, and I would bat their concerns away. I stayed away from school as much as I could and cut down on my socialising so that people wouldn't notice the way I was losing weight. I hated to feel looked at and watched, and I wanted to avoid situations where I might have to eat and drink in public, terrified of the fattening qualities of alcohol and of being observed while I ate.

Somehow, Jessica was fully aware of my new-found eating disorder. One night I heard a knock at my door and I opened it to see a pizza-delivery boy on the doorstep. Jess had ordered me some food, using the last of her grant to make sure I would eat something that week.

As I took the greasy box into my little flat, I was furious with her for sending me the pizza. She knew I was on a diet and yet still she tempted me. To ensure I couldn't give in and eat, I flushed the pizza bit by bit down the toilet and I never did thank her for her kind gesture.

I began seeing big changes in my body. My face slimmed first. It was like watching a piece of fruit decompose as it changed shape. My jaw line was suddenly visible, my cheekbones became more prominent and my eyes started to sink in their sockets. My changing body thrilled me. Now I'd had a taste of being slim, I wanted more. I wasn't happy with becoming just an average size, now I wanted to be the thinnest person in the world. I would see young girls in the street, no older than twelve, whose slender bodies had not yet developed into a woman's, and I envied them. Of course I knew in some deep part of my mind that it was wrong to think this way, but the urge to be thin had started to cloud my judgement severely.

Anorexia had taken hold of me. I wasn't interested in being with my friends any more – my new state of mind was entirely self-obsessed. No one round me could possibly realise what I was going through. They didn't really know me. They didn't know who I had become. They didn't know how it felt to hate their body so much, they would happily carve off chunks of their flesh if it would make them thinner. I didn't care that people were worried. How dare they be concerned now – had they been blind before? I felt in control for the first time ever, and I was morphing into the person I had always wanted to be. My clothes hung off me like rags and the constant hunger was making me high.

But as the weight dropped off and my dosage of laxatives increased, my schoolwork continued to suffer. I was still only attending classes just enough to keep on the right side of the authorities – who didn't seem to notice my condition – and I had lost all contact with the outside world.

I spent most of my time in my tiny flat, drinking cups of black coffee with sweetener. The stomach pains were still eating me alive, my hair and nails had stopped growing and I had a constant acidic taste of bile in the back of my throat from the lack of food. Crippled with pain in my bed and freezing cold, I would cry myself to sleep, hoping I would wake up the next day thinner. I wanted desperately to find the courage to call my mum and ask her to come and get me but I was afraid it would hurt her too much. What would she think when she saw her baby so ill and frail? How would she feel knowing her son, who was always so full of smiles and love, was slowly killing himself? My phone calls to Leicester became short and irregular. When I did speak to my mum, I masked my sadness with fairy tales of how wonderful Central was, telling her how happy I felt and what a good move coming to London had been. If she sensed there was anything wrong, I would convince her I was just tired and told her I loved her so very much. I was afraid that if the family got the slightest hint of the state I was in, they would appear in London at once and make me go back to Leicester with them, a failure. I couldn't let them see me like this. So I locked my door to the world.

By the end of that term, I had lost around four stone. My food diary reads:

Thursday, 14th March
1 apple, 1 banana and 40 laxatives.

Friday, 15th March
2 apples, 1 Slimma soup and 40 laxatives.

Saturday, 16th March
2 teaspoons of honey, 40 laxatives.

Sunday, 17th March
1 crisp bread, 40 laxatives.

Monday, 18th March
1 teaspoon of honey, 50 laxatives.

I was on the brink of starvation and yet I still wasn't satisfied. My ribs were plainly visible, my waist was a mere twenty-seven inches (a female size 8–10 and, believe me, on a man of six foot one, that's thin), and my head looked enormous on my skinny frame. But I still needed to be *thinner*.

It wasn't long before everyone round me was afraid of what they saw. They could see a radical difference in my appearance and they had noticed a shift in my personality. I had become withdrawn and private, and was no longer the life and soul of the party. Instead, I was sad and vacant, only half the boy who had arrived in London six months earlier. I wasn't interested in my friends, as I was too concerned with myself. Other people, no matter what their intentions, had become intruders and I had sunk ever more deeply into isolation, with only my obsession for company.

I don't remember going home that Easter break, but I must have done, because when the new term started, it was obvious that my family had become very worried about me. I began getting visits from my concerned brother and his wife, Lisa.

Kwok-Lyn and Lisa had met in Portsmouth when they were very young, just after my brother left college. After only a few months of courting, Lisa had packed up her pink suitcase and moved to Leicester to become the newest member of our family. Just as my mum had done in the late sixties, Lisa quickly adjusted to the Anglo-Chinese way of living and before long she, too, was a prawn-cracker-packing expert as she settled into the family coop and our hearts.

Kwok-Lyn and Lisa would come to London on their days off from the restaurant and feed me. In the days before they arrived, I would take in excess of one hundred laxatives to prepare for the next day of eating. Determined to convince my family I was okay, I would use the anorexic's cunning of going along with my brother's kind intentions, spending his visits eating meal after meal, only to make myself violently sick or stuff myself with laxatives as soon as they had gone. I didn't feel guilty for deceiving him, as I was convinced that once I was a thinner person I would be happy and successful, and that would make my family happy.

When they couldn't visit, they telephoned and wrote to me. It became a constant line of communication – calls when my mother asked me plaintively about what I'd eaten and I tried to keep her happy by spinning stories of pizzas and takeaways, and she asked if I had enough money for food. There were streams of letters and cards reminding me that they were thinking of me all the time, and sending me their love and support.

A typical note from my mother read:

Dear Babe,

    I hope you enjoyed your pizza. Enclosed five pounds, not that it's very much but I'm not sure about sending money through the post any more. I wish I was rich so I could send you lots of money. I'll put a little in your bank on Thursday. Love you.

    Mum and Dad

I knew that they were desperate about me. Oilen tried to let me know that they were all aware of my condition in letters she sent me – funny, gossipy letters that joked about diets and anorexia but that actually revealed her anxieties for me.

The messages came thick and fast but although I was aware of the love they contained, they did nothing to alter the course I was on.

I started to become obsessed with my reflection. I would stand naked in front of the mirror and pull my sagging skin in ways that made me look thinner. I even wished I had the nerve to take a knife to my body and shred the mess I had created. One night I sat on my bed, naked, clutching my knees to my chest, rocking and sobbing, telling myself that the only time I'd feel happy being full again would be if I knew I would die the moment after.

I fantasised about killing myself – I could see no other way out. I hated my body and I hated who I had become. I was sure that the way I looked was responsible for my loneliness – but I also knew I was ill. I knew that I needed to eat food and that if I continued in this way, I would die. But I was terrified that if I ate, I would become fat again – and that would mean I had failed. I would rather die than fail any more. But I was tormented by my hunger and the need to eat. How could I escape this awful, vicious circle? After hours of soul-searching and many tears, I concluded that suicide was my only option.

But I never did try to kill myself. I was too scared. What if I didn't succeed at it? If I was found full of pills or in a bath of bloody water just before I had managed to die, then that would be just another failing. I was afraid people would think me crazy or stupid or, worse still, just looking for attention.

And so my hellish existence continued.

By early summer, I was emaciated. My collarbones were so deep, they collected water when I showered. My ribcage was poking through my clothes; my hip bones created creases in my trousers and my fingers were so cold, I could barely hold a cup. I had achieved my goal of losing weight – I had lost another two stone and it was still dropping off me – and although I believed that I wasn't yet thin enough, at least now I was starting to resemble my peers, as I saw it.

Perhaps due to this warped belief, something inside me woke up, and I decided I had to come out of myself enough to return to Central and give myself one last chance to succeed. I had been staying away because we weren't required in school so much by the third term, as we were doing a lot of work on our own – projects and assignments and revision time – but I knew I needed to get back on track if I was going to stay. So I pulled together what strength I had and went in.

I expected to be treated differently: maybe my new body was going to make my lecturers feel sorry for me and they would pass my coursework; or maybe I was going to be singled out by the acting department, and I would declared thin enough to be considered for their course. But, of course, I was treated no differently than

I had been before – I was still warned that I needed to pull my socks up if I was going to pass the course.

The third term was devoted to producing and performing a play at the Minack Theatre in Cornwall. It was a tradition at Central, the completion of the first year was always marked by the milestone of 'getting to the Minack'. The students spent the term in London devising, writing, directing and rehearsing the play before taking it down to Cornwall to perform. For the first time in ages, I felt excited. This was going to be my last chance to show off my performing skills.

I'd guessed by now that my fantasy of my lecturers begging me to change to the acting course had a less than zero chance of happening, but now I nurtured a different dream. I imagined a casting agent spotting me and offering me work in the West End. That would be my ticket out of Central – I wouldn't have to say I'd failed, I could just tell people I had got a better offer.

Work began on the play but within days my optimism had been shattered by not being cast in a lead role. Instead, I was set the task of designing and making a mermaid costume. I had only used a needle and thread once before, in a domestic science class at school years ago when I'd made a bunch of grapes out of fabric that had absurdly impressed my teacher.

Now I set to, creating a shimmering, beautiful costume. My brain was blinded by hunger and I have no memory at all of the costume, but according to Lydia, I took great care over it, sewing on hundreds of faux pearls with meticulous attention to detail. My memories are less of a glittering mermaid than of agonising stomach pains as I continued my laxative abuse and survived on just a few teaspoons of honey a day, occasionally allowing myself small mouthfuls of sustenance when I knew that without it, I might collapse altogether.

To make up for the disappointment of not performing a lead role, I was given a small part in the play. I was cast as a clawed monster, soon to be nicknamed the Lobster. This only made me more unhappy. I felt humiliated and embarrassed, concerned that my imaginary casting director would see me and not have any room on his books for shellfish.

After weeks of rehearsing and costume making, and the opening night just days away, we were in the final stage of the dress rehearsal before we packed everything up for the trip to Cornwall. I can't remember what caused it or sparked me off, but that day, something inside me just snapped. I couldn't take it any longer. I was tired and frustrated and I couldn't face the reality of failing yet again. I knew I had to get out. I would find something better. I would make it on my own, I told myself. I would never become an actor if I stayed here.

Moments before we began our final dress rehearsal, I called Helen, the tutor, to one side.

'I'm going,' I told her. 'I'm sorry to leave everyone in the shit, but I can't take it any longer. I'm going to try and make it on my own. I wish I could stay but I just can't do it.'

As I talked, I realised I was happier than I had been in weeks. Finally, I was being honest about how I felt, and it was amazing. I no longer had to be the fat kid who had failed. I could be the fat kid who walked out because he was too good for the school. I was disillusioned and scared but I had no choice. I knew in my heart I had to leave Central because I was dying. The place was killing me. I couldn't be trusted with my life as long as I was there.

Helen listened to what I said and, with the same glare she gave me on that first day of term said: 'All right, then. You'd better go immediately.'

'Can't I say goodbye to everyone?' I asked.

'I don't think that's appropriate. A quiet exit will be best. Just slip away.'

I pleaded for a chance to say farewell but she snapped, 'Just leave!'

I stared back at her for an instant and thought, *No, FUCK YOU. I deserve this.* From somewhere, I found the strength I needed. I walked away from her and yelled at the top of my voice, 'Cast meeting!'

The entire year gathered on the first two rows in the auditorium and I stood up in front of all of them and said, 'I am so sorry but I'm going today. I am sorry for leaving you and I will miss you all very much. I just can't do it any more. I wish you luck with the show and I'll be thinking about you. Goodbye.'

They stared up at me with a mixture of shock and bemusement but nobody replied. Then I turned on my heel, and the Lobster left the building.

Dear Kwok,

I miss you. I miss us. The hardest thing was to watch you fall in love with Lisa and begin a new life away from me. I know that is selfish and it wasn't because I didn't care for Lisa, it was because I have always needed you. There is nowhere in the world I feel safer than when I am with you. I am so proud to call you my big brother, my protector, my friend. You have achieved so much with your life, including being a great father. I sometimes look at your world and envy what you have. I know it's unlikely I will ever have children of my own but that's okay because you have brought two wonderful souls into my life, Maya and Lola. Thank you. I need you to know I will never stop being your baby brother and I am so grateful for the silent guidance you have given me throughout my life. I love you.

Babe x

Dad's Noodles

INGREDIENTS

1 packet of Doll Instant noodles (wanton flavour – brown
   packet) per person
Chopped, wafer-thin ham
A few leaves of iceberg lettuce torn into shreds
Finely chopped spring onions
1 fried egg, to serve

METHOD

Cook the instant noodles according to packet instructions. While they are cooking, place the ham, spring
onions and lettuce in the bottom of a large noodle bowl.
Once the noodles are cooked, pour over the ingredients
already in the bowl. Fry your egg and place on top of the
cooked noodles. Eat. Enjoy.

Recipe by: Poppa Wan

CHAPTER THIRTEEN

Home Again

I left Central that day and went back to my flat. I didn't want to leave London, not yet at least, although I knew that it was almost inevitable I would end up having to return to Leicester. But I couldn't face going back home to tell the family the truth and admit that I hadn't been able to stick my course. Even so, it was a huge relief to know that I didn't have to struggle on any longer. I was free of Central and that was a huge weight off my shoulders.

I wasn't free of the anorexia, however, and its effects were plain to see. The fat, wobbling, twenty-one stone me had vanished, and in its place was a new and odd-looking version. I was emaciated to the point of weirdness. In fact, I looked like a kind of alien. But it hadn't passed me by that the fashion was for minute girls with stick legs and arms, and boys who were concave-chested, thin and unusual-looking – size zero and 'heroin chic' had become the *look du jour.*

I knew I was never going to become an actor by the conventional route – Central had proven that – so I looked for any way in. At the time, many 'real' models were getting acting jobs so I decided I would try that route. I knew I could never be a fashion model in a glossy magazine, I was far too unattractive for that kind of work, but I thought there was a chance I could be a 'boy next door' model or an 'extra', the kind of actor you see in adverts or silently sipping cups of tea in the back of the café in *EastEnders.*

I got a friend of mine to take some pictures of me in model-style poses around Camden, looking moody and, I hoped, magnificent. I wore drainpipe jeans on legs that were now literally as thin as drainpipes, a t-shirt and a child-sized vintage denim jacket. My bovver boots looked comically enormous at the end of my spindly legs, but I was pleased that at last I could wear the kind of clothes I'd always wanted. I posed for black-and-white pictures in dark glasses, with a cigarette clamped between my lips.

I sneaked back in to Central to use the computer room and get a list of all the model agencies in London then, off I went, list in hand and my frankly awful pictures in a folder, pounding the streets. Naturally the agencies took one look at the photographs and said, 'No, sorry, your look is too quirky for us' – the gentle way of telling me to fuck off and get real. Rejection followed rejection and I felt knocked back once again. How the hell was I ever going to succeed at anything in life? No one wanted me. I was no good at anything – *arghhh!*

Except, of course, I was good at controlling my eating. I had relaxed my regime a little by now but I was still terrified of putting on any weight. Instead of surviving on honey and laxatives alone, I was existing on a diet of fruit – plums, cherries, anything that would go through me quickly and not put any fat on me – and I was still taking laxatives to help it all through. The sugar in the fruit was all that was keeping me going and the laxatives were continuing their destructive work on my insides, rotting away at my stomach lining. I was constantly tired and had almost no energy.

One day I was walking down Oxford Street clutching a bag of cherries. I'd eaten so many on an empty acidic stomach that I had to throw up at the back of House of Fraser (not quite as chic as throwing up behind Selfridges). I had been rejected by the agencies but I was behaving like a model anyway.

Finally, I sat alone in my flat and realised I couldn't do it any longer. I couldn't stay in London with no prospects and living the way I was. I simply couldn't manage it. One day I would collapse, or not wake up in the morning.

I called my mum and dad. I needed them. Would they take me home?

*

Back in Leicester, my family took one look at me and knew something was devastatingly wrong. They'd had their suspicions already, as my weight decreased so dramatically, and had been trying to urge me to take care of myself. They had guessed at the worst, but their suspicions were not confirmed until I arrived back, a tired, soulless skeleton.

My mother gasped when she saw me, and her eyes said it all, but nothing was said aloud. No one had the first clue how to handle this situation, or understood how or why it had happened, or even what it was – least of all me.

Except, perhaps for Oilen. Strong and forthright, she knew there was something serious going on. She marched me to her bedroom and demanded to know what was wrong.

I didn't have the strength to fight any more. I was exhausted and beaten. I'd failed and now I was killing myself.

'I can't do this any more,' I said, breaking down and weeping. 'I need help. I can't go on like this.'

'It's okay,' Oilen said, taking charge. 'We're going to see the doctor. Today. Right now.'

I felt a huge relief – my big sister was in control and I had the security around me of the people I knew would always care for me. Surely everything was going to be all right.

The *Reader's Digest* and *Woman's Realm* magazines I flicked through in the surgery waiting room were probably the same ones I'd looked at over the past decade.

It didn't matter. I wasn't looking to read anything. I had sat in this waiting room every time I had been ill for the past twenty-one years. The clean smell of disinfectant was comforting; whenever I had smelled this antiseptic sweetness, I'd known I was about to be cured. I was hopeful.

My bum went numb as I waited for my name to be called. I had lost so much weight, the bones in my backside were digging into the plastic chair; it was a satisfying feeling.

Oilen sat with me. She didn't speak, she just held my hand as though I was a small child again. I felt comforted. I knew she was there because she loved me.

Dear Oilen,

At times you've wanted to kill me and at times I thought you might have done. You've always been more than my big sister; you have been the brain of our family and only age can help me write this letter to you, but I want to say thank you because if you had not been with me that day, then I might not be able to write this to you now. I love you, Oilen, and thank you for always being my idol.

Babe x

When we were finally called into Dr Kabra's room, Oilen stood behind my chair with her hand on my shoulder. The room was silent, except for the rustling sound of the doctor shuffling my medical notes as he looked through them. I was tired and my eyes were stinging from the hours of crying I'd been doing since arriving home. My stomach ached from yesterday's laxatives but I knew I was doing the right thing.

'Now, what's wrong with you?' Dr Kabra said at last, looking up. 'How can I help?'

'I've been dieting for seven months,' I said haltingly. 'I've lost nearly ten stone in weight, but I'm afraid that I'm an anorexic. In fact, I know I'm an anorexic. And I'm addicted to laxatives; I'm taking dozens a day. But I know I'm killing myself and I don't want to be this way any more.'

As I finally spoke it all aloud, I thought I might cry again, but I didn't. Everything I told the doctor he could see with his own eyes. He had known me since the day I was born and had watched me gain weight at the age of four and continue to get fatter and fatter. The more I spoke, the heavier Oilen's hand felt on my shoulder until it began to dig into my collarbone, but I was too numb to feel any pain.

'Take off your shoes and stand on the scales,' was the doctor's reply. I did as he asked, but looked away. I didn't want to see how much weight I'd lost. It was just too painful. I was ashamed of what I had become.

Before we left his consulting room, the doctor began to write in my notes. I sat, watched and read: 'I suspect Kowkhyn Wan to be suffering from anorexia.'

It was like a punch to the stomach. He didn't believe me. It was only *suspected*. Had I failed again? Could I not even do this right?

He didn't suggest a course of treatment or anything other than I start eating more food (I could have come up with that remedy myself). Oilen took us home.

Mum was waiting for us anxiously. As we walked through the door, I broke down in tears like I'd never done before in front of my mum, and told her what I'd told Oilen that morning – I didn't want to be like this any more, I didn't know what I was doing or why, and I didn't know how to stop, either.

Mum cried and cried. She held me in her arms and as much as I needed her, I didn't want her to hold me, I didn't want her to feel my bones. It was terrible. For the first time ever, her embrace didn't feel right. I felt disgusting – I wasn't the child that she used to cradle. I was someone different now, someone I didn't under-stand – someone no one understood.

For the first time I knew with absolute conviction that I had to get better.

CHAPTER FOURTEEN

Deep-fried Blues

My family began a dedicated mission to help me back to health. I don't know whether Oilen did some research on eating disorders and how to help an anorexic, but she became the matron of my recovery. Everyone did all they could to wheedle, beg and coax me to eat. Mealtimes were awkward and uncomfortable as the family watched me, counting every mouthful of food that passed my lips. I knew I had to eat but I hated the fact that every mealtime was like being at the zoo and I was the animal, being watched as every morsel passed my lips. No matter how much I ate, Mum was always pushing me, asking if I was hungry until I wanted to scream, 'Of course I'm hungry! How could I be anything else surviving on virtually nothing? But that doesn't mean I can eat!'

My anger wasn't directed at them; it was directed at myself and the voice of the disease that constantly told me I wasn't allowed food. I hated the anorexia for turning my mind against the people I cared about most.

I soon learned that no matter how often you push your food round your plate, it doesn't dissolve. Anorexics will always look for blame. I wanted to know why I was fat, why I overate and why I hadn't been able to control my eating when I was younger. If I'd only refused that second bowl of rice, maybe I wouldn't be here right now ... But I had to discover that food wasn't to blame; it wasn't my family, or my overeating. My anorexia had stemmed from my lack of self-worth, and self-esteem can't be bought from a supermarket or repaired overnight. I knew I had a long, hard slog ahead of me.

Mum tried to make eating times fun, as if I was a two-year-old again. She began to organise picnics and events where the food would be a part of the day, not the event. She even packed up the family car and made Dad drive us to a castle one day, and insisted I enjoy a picnic of cucumber sandwiches and salad. This was not typical of a Wan family picnic, usually filled with tinned ham and pickle cobs, Monster Munch and Cadbury's chocolate rolls. I knew she was making a special effort. Dad took a picture of Mum and me unpacking the picnic. I looked desperately ill as I stood by the picnic table, staring at food that I couldn't bring myself to touch.

The photograph should have frightened me, but instead I kept that picture to monitor how thin I was. I twisted the day that was supposed to help me and used it as an anorexic tool – if I stay this thin, I told myself, then I'm safe. I would look at it constantly as an aide to resisting food.

I really did want to get better and I was trying my best but it was very hard – nigh on impossible. I cut down on my laxative intake but I couldn't stop it entirely, and I couldn't break down the huge mental barriers I'd erected against food, especially against anything I considered fattening.

Meanwhile, The Panda had finally been laid to rest. The restaurant had been turned into a takeaway and Dad had rented it out to an Indian family who now ran a Balti house under our home. It made more sense for Dad to close his business and move it somewhere else for a fresh start, so he rented a place in Evington and set up a takeaway called The Gong, on the ground floor of a building with a flat above.

We all took up our positions in the new business. Dad was in the kitchen with Mum and Kwok-Lyn, while Oilen and Lisa worked the counter. I would float between the two but I quickly worked out that cooking all night gave me more opportunity to lose weight as I had to lift heavy woks in the sweltering heat. The huge industrial woks filled with rice were so heavy, they would take two hands to lift and the tendons in my skinny arms would look like they were about to snap as I heaved. It hurt but I was confident the strenuous work would keep me fit and keep my weight down.

London felt years away. It was if I had never auditioned at Central, never dressed up as a lobster and never had any ambitions to be an actor. I had done a full circle and I was back, working for Mum and Dad.

I had no problems in the kitchen. Dad had taught us all to cook when we were younger. He still sometimes insists we watch him and learn his skill – being able to cook is like a family heirloom in our clan. Over a couple of nights I watched Dad in the takeaway and got up to speed on the dishes on his new menu. More often than not, Dad would cook the more complicated dishes and I would be posted to the right of the range, tossing rice and frying the odd chow mein.

For so many years food had been my friend. It had kept me company when I was lonely and allowed me to share special times with the ones I loved. Food was my only connection with my dad's heritage, and it also allowed me to speak my dad's language. Not any longer, though. Food and I were through! Food was my sworn enemy, and oil was the biggest Judas of them all.

In the takeaway kitchen, I would watch Dad deep-fry the chicken balls and it would make me feel sick. The smell of boiling oil would make my stomach turn somersaults. When Dad laced the wok with oil, the sight of the hot, shiny fluid swishing round would bring bile to the back of my throat. When he made the curry sauce and poured ladles of oil into the vat, I was disgusted – it was like watching him pour in fresh blood from an open wound.

My brain had been re-programmed. It was a bit like when I'd made sets of rules to deal with my paranoia about being attacked, and convinced myself that only parts of the college were safe to walk around. Food now had its rigid protocols. Certain foods were safe and others were dangerous. I was so afraid of being fat again that I was prepared to go to any lengths to make sure it didn't happen; even lying to my family. By now I had started to eat again, not much, but enough to keep the glaring eyes off me at mealtimes. But the only way I could eat was with a huge amount of control. The main rule was that there could be no fat – everything had to be fat-free. Vegetables and fruit were okay but it was better if they were raw. I had completely cut meat, fish and most carbohydrates out of my diet, except sugar-free cereal. I would occasionally eat a small bowl of rice to satisfy my family's prying eyes. The rest of my food came from packets that listed exactly the number of calories, the grams of fat and carbohydrates and so on. Only when I was absolutely sure what was going in could I bring myself to let anything pass my lips. I wouldn't eat anything with more than a couple of grams of fat in it per one hundred grams, and would fill my hollow stomach with Slimma soups, fat-free yoghurts and dried fruit bars. If I needed a boost I would dip my finger into a jar of honey.

To this day, my mum still won't allow honey in the house.

Eating had become an obstacle course of dodging, weaving and abseiling past certain foods. In the take-away kitchen there was an enormous jar filled with mixed dried fruit and nuts. I would permit myself to eat the fat-free, low-calorie dried fruit, but I never let myself touch the oil-rich, forbidden nuts. Even though I yearned for them they were a big sin and I didn't dare risk surrendering to them.

Above the takeaway there was a disused and unkempt flat. I asked Mum and Dad if I could move into it. I could see they were worried about the prospect of letting me out from under their concerned gaze but they knew they could monitor my eating while the takeaway was open and they were there. I was able to point to the fact that I was eating a lot more, I was making strides, I was getting better – and I needed some independence. I don't know if they believed me but they decided it was best to let me go – well, semi-go. Perhaps they were worried that keep-ing me at home would make me ill again.

I moved into the flat, relieved to have my privacy again. I was far from better, of course, even if I was allowing myself a little more food, but I wanted desper-ately to be on my own again. Anorexia is a private illness, suffered in isolation, like self-harming. It is a way of controlling emotional pain, because the hungrier you are and the more you control what you put in your body, the more the pain is *owned and disciplined*. You can also forget the pain because your brain is slightly twisted – you're usually in a caffeine haze from all the coffee you drink to prop yourself up, or you're so hungry that your brain isn't working properly and you're constantly dizzy. I was falling over all the time, tripping up and not being able to do things, or collapsing with exhaustion, because my brain and body were so starved. But while I was managing my eating, I didn't have to feel my pain.

Now I was alone in the flat, some of that pain came back. I felt so low and such a failure and like I had nothing.

When the takeaway closed at 11 p.m, the family would all go home and I'd climb the stairs to the flat that smelled repulsively of fried food. I'd take out the letters that my family had sent me while I was in London – the dozens of letters and cards that told me how much they loved me and wanted me to take care of myself, and read them through, desperately trying to convince myself that yes, I was worth loving.

In the end, it was the love they sent me through the post that saved me. The paper might have discoloured and the ink faded, but the love and warmth was still carefully packed in the envelopes. I realised that being ill again was not an option, because they cared about me and I'd already put them through so much.

I knew that I wanted to go back to London, and that I couldn't go back unless I was better or it would drive my parents crazy with worry. I couldn't put them through it again. There was no intervention, no medicine, no counselling. There was just me, in my flat, reading those letters and telling myself I had to beat this. It was as if my heart woke up for the first time in twelve months and told me if I didn't change, I would die. The love from those letters told me I had more to live for than my disease. It was tough and lonely, but the battle had only just begun. What I didn't know was that my anorexia was like a parasite, lying just dormant below the surface, ready to come to life again. I would never be free.

Dear Mum,

I need you to know I love you so very much and I'm sorry I scared you. I never wanted to make you worry. This wasn't your fault and I need you to know I will never scare you again like that.

I love you.

CHAPTER FIFTEEN

Lacroix Meets the Boy Wan-der

I'd been back in Leicester for about a year when I had a call from Jessica, my friend from Central who had ordered me the pizza eighteen months before. Jess had met a guy called Matt and they were going to move in together. Did I want to come and be their flatmate? Quicker than you could say two egg-fried rice and a pancake roll, I was packing up my stuff at the takeaway and heading to Kingsbury, North London.

Moving back to London in 1996 was a simple decision as it offered so much more opportunity than Leicester. Although I had given up on drama school (there was no way I could return, battered, bruised and broken), I had not lost my dreams or ambitions. Performing was still the only thing I wanted to do. It was the only thing I *could* do. I just needed to make amends with my ego and stay strong, long enough, to give it one last shot.

My family was naturally concerned but they knew they had to let me go if I was ever going to get better. It was a double-edged sword: if I stayed in Leicester I would remain depressed, constantly reminded of my failure at Central, and more likely to slide back into my illness. But if I left for London, they would not be able to monitor my recovery. In the end, they had to let me go, but they did so on the understanding that I would return home as often as I could and I promised I would eat regularly.

Jess and Matt had found a two-bedroom flat in north London. It was small and unfurnished, and on the top floor of a purpose-built block with views of trees and playing fields. It was much grander than any place I had lived in before. Jess and Matt did a run to IKEA and kitted the rooms out with modern stainless steel, and a big sofa. Mum had given me a few pieces of furniture and I had somehow acquired a shop clothing rail that I used as my wardrobe. Our new home looked like a credit-crunch *Big Brother* house. It was perfect and I felt happy and excited to have such a positive new start.

By this time, Jess had also dropped out of Central. The strain of the course had made her question whether it was right for her. Her talent was singing and, like me, she would have been far better suited to the performance course. Instead, she had begun work as a receptionist at a beauty therapy company in Richmond. She was brilliant at it and managed the therapist's diaries with absolute precision, telling herself that it was just a pit stop while she waited for her big break – I knew one day she would be a big star ...

I decided I would look for work in Richmond, too, so that Jess and I could travel to work together and hang out at lunchtimes. I knew I needed to be round my friends if I was going to survive my second attempt at making it in London.

I managed to get an interview with Habitat and was called in for an interview. I had no retail experience but my interviewer must have liked me as I walked out with a position as a sales assistant in the furniture department, starting straight away. It wasn't glamorous and the pay was shocking but the staff was young, friendly and almost all of them were creative types. Some were budding designers, some had degrees in product design and some had studied textiles. It's sad how so much creative talent is hidden away behind till points, locked away in stockrooms and banished to the graduates' graveyard of British retail!

It didn't take me long to make new friends and it was where I met my best friend for life, E'lain-Ann.

E'lain has been my rock for the past fifteen years. She is funny, loyal, clever and, annoyingly, always right. She has the talent of being able to persuade you to see life differently; just when you think the arse is about to fall out of your world, she swoops in, full of silver linings, and repairs all the bad with a double handful of good. What a gal! E'lain is the cream in my coffee, the salt on my chips and the light in my darkness. My life would be so plain and lacklustre without her.

E'lain was born in Singapore but moved to the UK in the late eighties to study for her A levels, degree and Masters. The first day we met, three months after I had started there myself, E'lain was having an interview for a staff job at Habitat. I walked past the kitchen, backstage at Le Theatre du Habitat, and saw her through the glass window in the door. There she sat, beautiful and Oriental, with blood-red lips and dark wavy hair. She had a perfectly proportioned, hour-glass figure and real feminine allure. Although I couldn't hear what they were saying, I could tell E'lain was blinding her interviewer, my boss, with her charismatic charm. It was like watching a silent movie where the beautiful yet sinister *femme fatale* is about to claw her way into the man's heart. Her performance was worthy of a Habi-Oscar!

As I watched, desperate to know who this strange temptress was, I began to feel jealous and insecure. This was my patch. I was the exotic one whom everyone wanted to be friends with. For crying out loud, I was the resident Chink – there was no room for an invasion from Singapore!

To my horror, E'lain was offered the job and to boot, she was to work alongside me on the furniture department. Bollocks!

I was wary and a little chilly at first but it didn't take long for my initial suspicions to pass. E'lain proved herself to be great fun and we bonded completely. Soon we were spending most of our nights getting drunk in the local gay pub, the Richmond Arms. We earned so little money at Habitat that we would often sacrifice our lunch for a couple of pints in the evening. When we were really skint, we would go halves on a quarter bottle of cheap vodka, sneak it into the pub (often down E'lain's cleavage) and spend the night buying soft drinks to mix with our contraband.

It was the best summer of my life. E'lain and I claimed Habitat as our own. We would kid around, saying we were planning on re-branding the store into a mini Chinatown and threatening to hang roast duck and pork in the window, whilst changing the sign to read HAA-BI-TAA!

For the first time since leaving Central, I was feeling positive. E'lain's friendship gave me a reason not to hate myself. I was a good friend and I enjoyed hearing about her life and telling her about mine in return. I wasn't afraid to admit I had been sick. My confidence was rising and the more E'lain got to know me, the easier it became to admit I would probably never fulfil my dreams of being an actor. For now, it was enough to be a sales assistant and a new best friend.

Dear E'lain,
   Fish balls on sticks, red lipstick, naked back-ward rolls and dancing all night. Warmth, love and

acceptance. Your loyalty and support over the years has become one of the things I live for. You mean so much to me, writing alone doesn't seem to justify my love for you. Whatever the sadness and fear I feel, I know you will always guide me with deep thought and consideration. I will climb the highest mountain, just for you ...

Gok x

I was also feeling better about being in London. This time round I knew what to expect and I soon realised just how much the pressure of Central had stopped me from fully enjoying everything the capital had to offer.

Then, something brilliant happened.

By chance, Jess had met an A & R (artists and repertoire) guy from a record label. She had sung for him and he became interested in signing her up. She told him she came from a musical family and her sister Fliss was also a budding songstress, so he asked to meet her, too. Within weeks, Jess and Fliss had been turned into a girl group called Dynamo and they were shooting an 'unsigned' video.

It was amazingly exciting. This was Jess's big chance – it looked like her break had come. The record label hooked them up with a couple of guys, one on guitar and the other on keyboards. They were given a hair and make-up artist, and stylists, and were taken to top London restaurants for meetings.

I was happy for Jess but I was also jealous. How could it be this simple? Although I had become one of the top sellers at Habitat, I couldn't now help feeling that my life was heading down another dead-end path when I saw Jess's new success. I felt frustrated because I desperately wanted Jess to do well but I wanted my big break, too. While Jess was enjoying her success and the excitement of possibilities, I was catching the train each day to fluff cushions and fold away sofa beds.

In the lead-up to Jess's video being shot, the stylists and make-up artist started work on the girls. It seemed so very glam to have a team of people employed just to make them look more attractive. I had no idea what a stylist did so Jess explained it all to me. The girls' sound was poppy and they were hoping to attract a teenage fan base along the lines of the S Club 7 formula: a bright, breezy sound, trendy outfits, some cool dance moves and – hey presto – record sales.

A stylist had been briefed to come up with a young and accessible look for Jess and Fliss, but they felt that she'd interpreted the brief clumsily. The look didn't appeal to them, the clothes were bad and they were upset.

I saw an opportunity and convinced Jess to let me step in and style her and Fliss. I had never styled anyone before but I knew what Jess liked and was sure that I had quite good taste in clothes. I loved shopping and although I was skint, I spent ages rummaging in unusual stores, markets and charity shops, buying clothes like seventies polyester shirts and skinny jeans for my studenty, vintage-inspired look. I dressed a little younger than my age (and still do!), but that was partly because I'd lost ten years of dressing thanks to being fat. I was making up for lost time – *that's Peter Panache syndrome!*

The girls agreed to let me have a go – after all, I couldn't be any worse than their previous stylist – and the record label were amenable, so I set about coming up with a look.

Jess told me the stylist had borrowed clothes for them to wear from shops. How easy! I had no idea how to borrow clothes, but how hard could it be?

After fifteen years of working in fashion, I now know how difficult it is to get hold of clothes for celebrities to wear. Even if the look is for famous actors and musicians, it can be tough to borrow clothes if the label thinks that the celeb doesn't fit the brand. Most of the clothes a stylist can borrow will come from a press office – these are samples and are usually from the next season's collection. Very occasionally, a brand may allow you to borrow from shop stock (if the celeb is not press sample size 10), but this is risky. The clothes must be returned in a sellable condition, otherwise the stylist is liable for the full cost of the clothes.

I didn't know any of this back then. Instead, a few days later saw me strutting my way through the heavy doors of Harrods with one mission in mind: to dress Dynamo for their debut single.

I checked out every department in the store. I was looking for young and funky, accessible and fun. I didn't care what labels I looked at, it didn't matter how high end – Versace, Dior, Chanel – as far as I was concerned, stylists could just help themselves to whatever they wanted: no matter that the 'celebs' were a couple of unknown girls from Birmingham.

I finally decided on some outrageously loud pieces from Christian Lacroix. Yes, you heard it right, the *haute couture* designer from Paris who is one of the biggest names in the business and had dressed all the top A-listers in the world.

The conversation went something like this:

Gok: Hi, my name is Gok Wan. I am a fashion stylist and I'm working with a new band called Dynamo on their video. I would like to borrow these clothes for the two lead singers to wear. (Hands over huge pile of clothes.)

Sales girl: Erm ... okay. Let me just speak with my manager. Have you made an appointment with our press office in Paris?

Gok: Oh ... No. (Smiles nervously.)

Sales girl: Wait there one moment, please, while I call my manager. Thank you.

The girl sashayed off, vanishing through a door hidden in the department's mirrored walls. As I stood waiting, I began to panic. Shit, she's going to think I'm a thief! What the fuck is a press office? Jess said her stylist had just borrowed the clothes, no one said anything about a fucking press office!

Within moments the sales assistant had reappeared, but she wasn't smiling.

Sales girl: Hi. Do you have a business card?

Gok: Um ... No. (Now blushing like a thief caught red-handed.)

Sales girl: Do you have a letter from the record label?

Gok: Er ... No. (Desperate for a hidden door in the mirrors just for me!)

Sales girl: Excuse me one moment.

She vanished into her mirror once again. I was now so panicked my anxiety was making me sweat. I couldn't just run out of the door, could I? Surely the security guards would stop me, mid-escape, and I would be arrested for trying to pull a fast one!

It was then that four years of drama training suddenly wasn't such a waste of time. As the girl returned, I decided I was going to take control of the situation. There was no way I was going to leave the store without these clothes. This was my one opportunity to get involved with the band. Before the sales

assistant could open her Chanel-lipstick-coated mouth,
I began my pitch:

Gok: Okay ... I am so sorry about this. I have just
spoken with my A & R guy at the label and it
would appear there has been some mix up.
My assistant should have called your press
office but we are so behind deadline with the
video, the phone call never happened. The
band is flying in from Japan this afternoon
and unless I have these wonderful clothes, I
am going to be in deep trouble. Can I suggest
you take a print of my debit card ... (Hands
over a card with about £4 on it)... and if
there's a problem, then you can just ring the
clothes through for the full amount?

The sales assistant looked surprised. I began my closing speech:

Gok: I know this is not what usually happens but
the band and the LABEL have specifically
requested Lacroix so I don't want you to get
into trouble, either! Can you please make an
exception, just this once? (The biggest smile
fills my face. Long pause.)
Sales girl: Okay. I'll do it this once but you will have to
make sure that when you want to borrow

clothes in future, it's agreed with the press office.

Gok: Oh my God! Of course!

I couldn't believe I had done it! I literally skipped out of Harrods with tens of thousands of pounds worth of clothes in my arms.

Little did I know that, in years to come, this would be the way I earned my living.

CHAPTER SIXTEEN

Colourings In

W ell, it seemed a stylist wasn't born in a day. The clothes proved not to be right for the record label and so they were returned to Harrods unworn. And in a perfectly sellable condition, thank Christ!

Unfortunately, the single didn't do very well so Jess remained working at the beauty salon. It was a great experience and I don't think Jess regretted it, but I will always feel that her talent was wasted.

As the summer rolled by, I started to spend more time with E'lain and stayed at her place more than I did at my own flat in Kingsbury (we would sit up all night watching *Queer as Folk* in her bed, eating pizza and guzzling cans of beer – bliss!). It was partly because E'lain lived in Richmond, which meant I could save my travel money for nights out, and partly because I was feeling a little uncomfortable living with a couple.

At the same time, Habitat was becoming a bind. I wanted so much more from my job. I loved the people I worked with and E'lain made the days fun and exciting, but I knew I couldn't stay working there on a crappy wage with no career prospects.

The more restless I felt, the more I would control my eating. I was still very thin, although I had stabilised my weight at a reasonably healthy ten and a half stone (up from my lowest of nine stone), and whenever I felt I was not achieving anything I would still begin to decrease my food intake and control which foods I would permit myself to eat.

I knew I had to leave Habitat because if I didn't then I would end up starving myself again, and the anorexia would take hold once more.

Below Jess's beauty salon was a branch of The Body Shop. Jess had made friends with the manager, Donna, and suggested I speak to her about a job. During Jess's brief musical career, I had watched her get her make-up done and was fascinated at how easy it looked and what skilfully applied make-up could achieve. A couple of times I had suggested to Jess that I should do her make-up before we went out, and with her careful guidance I had not done a bad job. I'd also learned how to apply stage make-up at Charles Keene when performing in *Cabaret* in my final year, so I knew the basics.

As it happened, the Richmond Body Shop was advertising for a make-up specialist to help sell the range, as well as do makeovers in store. I had a meeting with Donna, assured her – with my usual drama-school blag – that I had loads of experience, and was offered the job as Richmond Body Shop's 'Colourings' expert.

I said goodbye to Habitat without much regret, though of course I was going to miss working with E'lain. Something told me that I might be able to find my way to a career this way that suited me more than by carrying on in the soft furnishings arena.

I liked my new job at once. The Body Shop was so different to Habitat; it was small, personal and I felt at home there – perhaps I was just more interested in make-up than in sofa beds. Within a couple of weeks I had a thriving make-up stand. I employed my customer service skills learned in Dad's restaurant, my acting skills from drama school and my new sales skills from Habitat, and before long I was doing makeover after makeover every day. It felt great.

The make-up I was doing was pretty basic and I was almost completely self-taught. I would always read glossy fashion magazines in Jess's beauty salon, so I knew what the new trends and latest looks were, and my natural eye for colour and what worked with what helped me. And despite my lack of expertise, the customers liked me. I made them feel warm and beautiful. I laughed with them, listened to their problems, advised them on their relationships and in return they bought my make-up. My career, as I knew it, had begun.

I grew to love the job. I was in charge of the stand, the ordering, merchandising, cleaning and, of course, the selling. I thrived on the responsibility. For the first time I felt I had a proper job and that gave me a sense of importance, which was quite new.

While work was going from strength to strength, my home life in Kingsbury, however, had become strained. I loved Jess but I felt as if I needed to spread my wings. It was hard to live with a couple. I would spend most of my time at E'lain's place or in my bedroom, as I didn't want to impinge on Jess and Matt's 'together' time. Matt had a high-powered job and Jess was working hard at the salon so it was only right they wanted their evenings to cuddle on the sofa and be a couple. It must have been hard with a six-foot Chinese flatmate mincing round!

I had earned very little money at Habitat and The Body Shop wasn't a great payer, either, so most of my wages went on travel, food and the occasional night out. As a result, I began to fall behind on my rent, which I now know wasn't fair on Jess and Matt and I realised I was going to have to find somewhere cheaper to live. I asked Mum and Dad to bail me out and then told Jess I was leaving. It was a hard decision, as Jess had become my

London family, but I couldn't stay when I couldn't pay my way.

Needing a place to go, I called Emma, my old friend from Central. Emma lived in Camden with her daughter, Ella, and her sister, Kathy. Emma was a few years senior to me and at Central she'd always seemed rather mysterious, perhaps because she was older and already had a life in London. Her friends were successful and creative and she seemed so sorted. Her life hadn't been a bubbling hotpot of mess like mine; she just got on with things. Perhaps it was the fact Emma was a mother that made her seem more settled, but whatever it was, I looked up to her and Emma's world had been a nice break from the stresses of college.

I explained my situation to Emma and she immediately offered me a cheap, short-term let of Ella's room while I got my act together. Ella didn't mind bunking in with Mum. I accepted gratefully and packed my bags again.

Dear Jess,

I miss you. You cared for me when I needed it most and I will always be indebted to you for that. I am gutted we went our separate ways but I want you to know how special you are in my memories.

Gok x

Camden was great fun and I loved living with the girls. The flat was big and spacious. Emma and Kathy came from a middle-class hippie family, and the flat was always a little untidy but the mess didn't bother me. I was staying in a comfortable family home with routines, security and no rules except, 'Don't leave the hot water on'.

Emma was always on hand for a heart-to-heart. She was still at Central and doing very well; she was academic and enjoyed the theory classes more than the practical, so the course was just right for her. She was a great friend to me, helping to alleviate my loneliness, supporting me and making me feel like one of the family. I got on well with Kathy, too, and six-year-old Ella and I had a great friendship that consisted mainly of me dressing her up and doing her hair. I was her Auntie Gok.

It was while I was living in Emma's flat that I finally came out to Mum and Dad.

It started with one of the days my sister and brother came to visit. It was the middle of the summer in my second year in London. Because of my illness, Oilen and Kwok-Lyn were still making sure that they came often to London to check up on me. Their visits were mainly to make sure that I was eating, but also to fill me in on family gossip and hear what I'd been up to. That day, I wasn't in a great mood. Maybe I had a hangover or maybe I was just not up for food monitoring that day, but the visit was subdued and I was quieter than normal. As I said goodbye to Oilen and Kwok-Lyn on the flat balcony, Oilen said to me, 'You'd be happier if you came out to Mum and Dad.'

Her statement knocked me for six. I had wanted to tell Mum and Dad I was gay for a long time but I was held back by the fear that I might lose them. I suppose I knew deep down Mum and Dad would understand, but there was still a risk they wouldn't and it was one that I wasn't prepared to take. Mum and Dad had given me so much. They had cared for me all my life, nursed me when I was sick, clothed and fed me, forgiven me, loved me and they had helped me through my anorexia. How could I tell them I was gay? What if Dad, with his strong sense of Chinese traditions, couldn't cope with it? What would his brothers say? How could I let my dad down and make him the black sheep of his family just because I fancied boys? The thought of waking up one day without the support and security of my family made me despair. They had always been everything to me and life without them was too miserable to contemplate.

'No,' I said firmly. 'Absolutely not. I'm not ready to tell them yet. I will one day, but not right now.'

Later that evening the telephone rang. It was Mum. I took the phone outside to the small balcony and sat down with it. Mum's voice was unusually quiet and apprehensive. I asked her what was wrong.

'Nothing,' she replied. 'The kids are home.'

'Oh, great. That's good.' I started to reel off what we had done that day but she stopped me mid-sentence.

'I know,' she said simply.

'You know what?' I said.

'I know you're gay.'

Silence.

I was mortified. My eyes filled with tears and I began to cry. I couldn't speak. It was too soon. I wasn't ready. I thought: I need my family and now they're going to hate me. Dad will think I'm a freak, disgusting, abnormal ...

Suddenly the sunny balcony in Camden seemed like the loneliest place in the world. For a moment it wasn't the middle of the summer, kids weren't playing in the street and I no longer had a place in my family. My entire world had stopped turning and my heart sank into my boots.

Finally, Mum spoke. 'It's okay. I still love you. Don't worry, Babe, you'll always be our son.'

I still couldn't speak. I hated my mum saying this to me. Why was she being so nice when I was the one in the wrong? It wasn't her fault I was a freak! She was the innocent party and yet she spoke as if *I* had to forgive *her*!

I found the courage to speak. 'Don't tell Dad ... Please ...'

I couldn't stand not having Dad's approval. I had already nearly ripped my family apart by starving myself and now I was about to take Dad's world and set fire to any pride he had left.

Mum said, 'I won't tell Dad yet ... but he will need to know.'

We sat in silence as the tears rolled down my face. I stared over the balcony into the streets of Camden Town for what felt like eternity, Mum on the other end of the phone.

You can't prepare yourself for coming out. There are no words of wisdom anyone can give you because coming out to your parents is such a solitary and personal experience.

It actually makes me angry that anyone should have to come out. My sister never pulled me to one side and told me quietly that she was straight. Nan never had to risk losing her family because she had fallen in love with a man. Why do gay people need to spend their teenage years preparing themselves for the risk of losing the people they love the most? It seems so unfair.

I was lucky because I knew my mum would love me no matter what, and I already knew that my brother and sister would stand by me. But Dad was another matter entirely and I was sick with fear over what his reaction would be.

A week later Mum called and said she had told Dad. He was okay, she said, and coming to terms with it. I knew I should have gone home to see him. But I was so afraid of having to face him, I pretended I was too busy to come home right away. I decided it was simpler to avoid contact and so I didn't go home for a long time after my coming out.

CHAPTER SEVENTEEN

Midnight Dash

After a while, I decided I had outstayed my welcome at Emma's. She had been so kind to let me stay but Ella needed her room back so I packed my bags again, and moved out.

During my time at The Body Shop, I had made friends with my boss. Donna was a feisty Irish lesbian who had moved to London a few years back when she'd fallen in love with an area manager. Donna and her lover had bought an ex-council flat in a high-rise block in Southfields. The building was dingy and unkempt but it had the best views of London I had ever seen. On a clear day you could see Wimbledon Common, which just about made up for the smell of piss in the lift.

The girls had recently separated and Donna asked if I wanted to move in while I saved some money. She knew I'd come unstuck with my rent in Kingsbury and that I'd left Emma's, so she allowed me to live with her rent-free. I think Donna was more in need of company than she was of hard cash.

My time in Southfields was drunken, debauched and fun. Donna and I explored the London gay scene together, tanked up on cans of Stella. We partied all over the city and made friends wherever we went. We became a well-oiled friend-making machine that no one could resist. There was never a short supply of party invites: if we didn't go to them, then they came to us, and Donna's flat would often be littered with empty cans and full of laughter. Soon, I'd settled into my temporary new home very nicely.

Dear Old Friends,

Growing apart is sad. Not a day passes when I don't think about you. We may have argued, we may have fought, but I have never not loved you. You know who you are.

Gok x

I had done so well with my make-up stand in Richmond that the area manager decided she wanted me to take my formula to some other stores. I would not only be the resident make-up artist in Richmond; I would start visiting the stores in Putney, High Street Kensington, Portobello Road and Whiteleys as well as Richmond, one for each day of the week.

I was buzzing at my new job prospects. It felt as if I was climbing the career ladder at a ridiculous rate and I decided that being a make-up artist was going to replace my ambition of being an actor.

My make-up skills had improved with practice and I was beginning to feel confident that this was a profession that would make me happy. I loved meeting new people and getting on well with my customers: I liked getting close to people and hearing about their lives. I had a natural skill for working out colours and using products, and I found sales very easy. My new job seemed like the perfect progression. Fired up with enthusiasm, I began to race round the city, working every day in one of my five stores.

It was hard work. I had to bond with a different team in each store, and each store manager had their own take on how the shop should be run. Most managers saw me as an asset and welcomed me, but others saw me as an intrusion, almost a company spy. They couldn't understand why I had been given such a huge lift up the ladder with the freedom to swan round the city answering to no one but the big bosses. They had no idea that I was still on the same wage as when I had started with the company, and that the swanning I was doing was adding ten hours of travelling time to my working week!

Not only that, it was lonely being on the road. I soon missed the companionship of working with the same people every day. It was difficult to build a relationship with new colleagues when I only saw them once a week, and I'd often miss out on team drinks and bonding get-togethers when people let their hair down, had a laugh and got to know each other.

It was also harder to build a client base in the more central parts of London. I hadn't realised Richmond was, in effect, a village where customers were loyal and friendly. My central London stores were much busier, but the customers were mostly tourists and passersby who didn't have time for a Gok makeover, no matter how hard I smiled!

My sales figures began to drop off dramatically. What had been a success story suddenly turned into a nightmare. I tried my best but nothing seemed to work. The worse I did at my new job, the more my confidence took a knock. Just as everything was going so well, I had made a wrong turn, and I started to panic. I was desperate to tell my boss I wanted my old job back, but my ego wouldn't allow me to admit I had made a mistake. I knew I was staring failure in the face again, and I couldn't bear the way that felt.

In the midst of all this, I decided I wanted to take back some control in my life.

Of all things, I decided it was time to introduce my family to my lover.

Ever since my parents had learned the truth about my sexuality a few months before, I had refused to go home for a visit. I was too embarrassed. It felt like Mum and Dad now had confirmation I was no longer a virgin and would look at me differently. I felt exposed and dirty.

My main worry was that this would be the first time that I'd seen Dad since he found out. Would he refuse to hug me? Would he be sickened at the mere sight of me? Would he ask how gay men have sex? I calmed down a bit when I realised that Dad had never discussed his sexuality with me – something for which I was glad about, if only for the sake of my lunch staying down – so why would I have to discuss mine with him?

Mum had reassured me that Dad was fine with my being gay, but she had always been a peacekeeper and I knew that her words perhaps couldn't be trusted.

I had started to date a guy whom I shall call Jason. Jason was sweet, pretty and he made me feel attractive. We had a healthy, enjoyable relationship hanging out, drinking and talking together, and the intimacy was good, too.

Although I had started to feel better about my body, I was still coming to terms with my new shape. It was sometimes a shock to look in the mirror and see a slimmer and, in places, bonier body rather than the fleshy blob I'd known for twenty-one years. Jason allowed me to forget I used to be fat and I revelled in the physical attention he gave me.

He had introduced me to his parents and it'd got to the point where I felt I should repay the compliment. So, one evening I rang him and told him to pack a bag. 'We're doing it! We're going home.'

Within an hour we were hurtling up the M1, on our way to Leicester.

We arrived at my parents' house at midnight. Mum and Dad had been working in the takeaway all night and, along with the rest of my family, were sitting at the kitchen table about to eat their evening meal when we walked in.

As we entered the kitchen, the tapping of chopsticks stopped as every head turned towards the door – even the dog's. There was a brief moment of silence as everyone stared at us in shock. My heart was racing out of control but I knew I had to remain cool for the sake of my sanity, as well as for Jason. As the initial shock wore off, the tapping resumed and my mother welcomed us nervously to the table, saying, 'Come in ... Get a bowl ... Are you hungry?'

I sheepishly introduced Jason to my family and we sat down to eat.

Usually mealtimes at The House of Wan are like feeding time at the zoo. There is always laughter, smiles, sharing of food and a genuine appreciation for the meal, but this time it was different. We ate in a deathly silence, without eye contact and with an awkwardness that frayed every single one of my nerves.

The quieter it became, the more I knew I had made a big mistake. This was so unfair on Dad. He hadn't seen me since he'd discovered I was gay and now I had surprised him at *his* dinner table, at midnight, with a lover! I felt guilty and stupid. I also felt guilty about Jason. He'd been brought into my family home under false pretences, tempted by a home-cooked meal in order that I could use him as a shield against my dad's possible disapproval.

After what felt like forever, we finished our meal: the centre serving plates had been cleared, leaving a scattering of rice over the table, yet still there was silence.

Then Dad stood up and left the room. This had never happened before. Dad was always the last to leave the table and *always* the last to finish eating. It was a Wan family tradition.

I exchanged awkward glances with Oilen, Kwok-Lyn and Lisa, then looked towards Mum, who shrugged her shoulders and raised her eyebrows with an expression of, 'I don't know!'

Fortunately, Jason had no idea this was out of character for my dad and innocently continued balancing a straw mushroom on his chopsticks.

After a few minutes I found the courage to leave the table to go in search of Dad, leaving Jason at the table. As I walked through the flat, I could hear Dad fumbling round in the living room. I stood at the door, watching him tuck a sheet over a makeshift bed on the floor. In the corner of the room the open fire had been stocked with fresh coal and there was the soft glow of a new flame. It was a sign. Dad had built Jason and me a bed to sleep on and lit a fire to keep us warm. In his own special way, he was telling me I was still his son and he still loved me. He had accepted me as I was.

Dad and I never discussed what being gay meant. He never asked me how two men have sex together, he never told me I was a freak and he continued to hug me as he had since I was a baby. Years later, he did tell me he didn't understand it, but he would always love me.

That was enough for me.

Puttanesca Sauce

INGREDIENTS

Large bag of dried pasta (you choose the style)
1 tin of chopped tomatoes
1 tin of anchovies in oil
20 chopped black olives
1 tablespoon of capers
2 fat cloves of garlic
Olive oil
Black pepper
1 lemon
Handful of fresh basil

METHOD

Boil the pasta in a large pan of salted water. Heat a wok or large-ish frying pan. Add oil, chopped garlic and anchovies. Mash the little bastards up with the back of a ladle. Add the tomatoes, black olives and capers; bring to a simmer and reduce the sauce. Drain the pasta and add the sauce, mixing up casually with a pout and guzzling down a can of beer. Ladle into a large pretentious serving bowl and add a good handful of fresh basil and a squeeze of lemon. Eat on your lap, making sure you get the sauce all down your chin and over your clothes. Once eaten, leave the dish at the side of the sofa and pass out feeling full and content. Enjoy.

CHAPTER EIGHTEEN

Platinum Coffee Table

With one great part of my life sorted out at last, I could finally relax a bit more. But my career was causing me grief. I was still running round London, doing Body Shop makeovers in my five outlets, but the constant battle to keep my stand busy was wearing me down and I knew it was time to leave.

I had decided that I was going to try and make a proper career out of make-up but I didn't want to stay in retail. I wanted to be a professional make-up artist and I was gunning to play with the big boys. So I called Ameneh.

Ameneh and I had met on a very drunken night in the student bar at Central. She was two years above me at the school, and one of the brightest students there – bitch! Half Persian and half English, Ameneh stood at a very proud five-foot nothing, had a killer smile and a laugh so dirty, it could make Bernard Manning turn in his grave. Armie and I got talking and when we realised the bar was closing, I invited her back to my bedsit for a drink (I must ask her if she thought I was offering her sex). We spent about four hours lying on my single bed drinking cheap wine, laughing, talking bullshit and sniffing a bottle of poppers. We instantly connected and by dawn, a true friendship had been cemented under a cloud of amyl nitrate, resulting in a two-day headache and a lifetime of best friend companionship. Later in life, she gave me a beautiful goddaughter, Yasmine. *Thank you, darling!*

I knew Armie had an old school friend who worked at *You* magazine, the supplement of the *Mail on Sunday*, so I asked her if she would put us in touch. Ameneh gave me the number for Kelly, who was just starting to make it as a lifestyle journalist. I called her and after a brief chat, she agreed to meet me for a coffee.

Kelly was incredibly helpful. We talked for an hour and I told her I'd done lots of make-up jobs and was just starting to build up my client list (I didn't tell her the only make-up I'd done was on the counter at The Body Shop!). Kelly gave me a list of names of stylists she had met on the magazine and told me that these were the people I should contact, as they were usually responsible for booking make-up artists for photo shoots. One person she recommended in particular was Sally Simpson.

Kelly told me that Sally was a very experienced commercial stylist, working mainly for the weekend supplements, like *You* magazine. She knew absolutely everyone in the business and was very well respected for her work. WOW!

As soon as I'd finished my meeting with Kelly, I called Sally. I was scared and excited in equal measures but had a strong feeling that this could be my way in. Sally was very charming and invited me to her apartment the following day for a meet and greet.

I was finally on the right track and if all went well, I hoped I'd be able to jack in my job and do professional make-up full time. That would be miles better than The Body Shop and even better than acting! Who wanted to slave round the country in a battered old tour bus with some egocentrics in a two-bit theatre company anyway? Darling, I work in *fashion*!

The next day I marched up to St John's Wood to meet Sally at her home. Her apartment was absolutely gorgeous, just how I'd imagined a stylist's home would be: totally cool and elegant with Rolls-Royce-precision style. It was split over two floors of a Victorian terrace conversion. The walls were painted brilliant white and over the fireplace hung the biggest mirror I had ever seen. Two luxurious white sofas faced each other over a table made of glass and what looked like platinum. The table had been accessorised with oversized photographic books and on every available surface were antique picture frames displaying the wonderful life of Sally Simpson.

Sally was amazing and she thrilled me. She had a neat page-boy haircut, wore black in such a way that I knew it was her everyday uniform (with perhaps a subtle shade of grey for special occasions) and had a magnificently gravelly voice thanks to her committed smoking of forty Silk Cut every day. I was sure I could guarantee a pair of black designer sunglasses would always be perched on the end of her button nose whenever she set foot outside. She was straight out of an episode of *Ab Fab*!

Sally was very gracious. She offered me a drink and asked me to sit down on one of the luxurious sofas. I was nervous and sat so close to the edge of the seat that with the smallest of misjudgements I would have toppled off on to her obviously outrageously expensive shagpile.

Three fags, a shot of espresso and five nervous twitches later, I was beginning to relax as we chatted. Who was this woman? Why the hell had I not met her before? She was amazing! Sally was warm and kind and didn't seem to mind me lusting over her wonderful career. She made no secret of her success as she proudly ran through her list of clients, telling me anecdotes from shoots and juicy stories of famous celebrities. The meeting was so unbelievably glamorous, all I could think was: *When I grow up, I want to be her!*

I told Sally that I hoped to break into the world of make-up and she was very encouraging. We hit it off very well and after a couple of hours I left her home feeling confident, charged and more ambitious than ever. Sally was definitely a role model for me. She was controlled, successful, renowned for her job and effortlessly fabulous! I skipped out of St John's Wood, happy I'd made a new contact and a potential new friend.

Within a week Sally had called and told me she had been asked to cover a maternity leave position as fashion editor for a leading women's weekly magazine. She would be shooting at least one fashion story a week, as well as any celebrity features that needed styling. She told me she was very interested in seeing what my make-up was like and gave me four jobs there and then. FUCK ME!

I was so taken aback I lost myself for a moment and agreed to all the shoots, not considering the fact that the only experience I had was on a make-up counter at The Body Shop. But it didn't take long for the reality to kick in and I panicked. I was being given an amazing opportunity and I didn't have the tools to do the job.

Most make-up artists have thousands of pounds worth of products in their kit – some bought and some given to them by public relations people in exchange for a credit in the magazines; very occasionally an artist will be sent a bag full of products to pass on to their celebrity clients.

I had no celebrity clients and I had not done any work for magazines at all. My kit comprised a shabby old B&Q

toolbox Dad had given me, filled with samples stolen from The Body Shop. There was no way I could rock up to a photo shoot with it ... How embarrassing!

Once again, the actor inside me took over. I rang Sally back and said I was so happy she liked me and I was excited about our first job together, but there was a problem. My kit had been stolen while I was on a job abroad and I was in the process of replacing it. I felt terrible for lying but I couldn't see any other way. Sally was great. She listened and although I'll never know whether or not she believed me, she asked me to meet her the next day in town as she wanted to introduce me to a friend of hers who ran the press office for a leading high-end make-up brand.

The next day I cleared up! We waltzed into a press office in Mayfair and, with my acting training, I managed to blag thousands of pounds' worth of make-up for my new kit. I couldn't believe it. From having virtually nothing, I now had more make-up than I knew what to do with.

Within a matter of weeks, I'd handed in my notice at The Body Shop, and Sally and I were working together. My make-up skills weren't the best, and I think Sally soon guessed that I'd exaggerated my experience, but she liked me and let me learn on the job. She knew what I could do and so she never asked me to perform a make-up miracle. Instead, she was happy for me to produce natural, nude looks, even if it didn't suit the shoot, and I didn't attempt anything too off-the-wall because I didn't dare experiment at this stage when the pictures were for publication. I simply couldn't risk messing up, so I played it very safe and Sally didn't seem to mind.

It was also great to finally be earning some proper money. I invoiced £220 for a day's work. Some weeks we would do three shoots, which earned me more money in one week than in a month from Habitat or The Body Shop. Kaaa-ching!

I also began to learn masses about people, celebrities, photographers and myself on these shoots. With every job I did my confidence grew. My hunger to be an actor was suppressed by my new-found career and passion – make-up. I didn't need retail, and this was far more glamorous.

It was also on these shoots that I learned how to be a stylist. I would watch Sally go through the whole process of styling, from reading a brief in which the editor described the ideas, emotions and look that was required for the shoot, to making the appointments with press offices to select clothes, and finally styling the job, shooting the pictures and returning the gear. I didn't know it then but I was learning the job that I would come to love.

On a couple of occasions, when I wasn't needed for make-up, Sally asked me to assist her. I loved it. I would go with her to the press appointments and watch her carefully select garments from huge rails of clothes. She would skilfully sweet-talk the press officers into loaning her more pieces than she was allowed, and I loved how she made it look so easy – in reality this is the hardest part of a stylist's job, especially when some of the PRs can be as prickly as a Durian fruit.

I watched her dress the models or celebrities on set, and she would make them feel gorgeous with constant reassurances: 'You look fabulous, darling!' or 'You must get this piece when it's out next season, it looks divine!' She created wonderful looks with accessories, transforming clothes with belts, jewellery, a certain kind of stocking or a fabulous pair of shoes. She could add a hat or brooch or a pair of gloves, and make the whole thing look fantastic. I loved seeing Sally work her styling magic. She was my mentor and I was her faithful protégé!

Over the next six months, I explored this new world with Sally's help, but sadly it didn't take long for me to realise that I was in another dead-end alley. I'd found a world that I loved working in but I was never going to make any progress. I wasn't improving my make-up skills and even though she'd been so kind to me, Sally couldn't provide me with an entire career. She was my only contact in the industry and I wasn't able to spread my net any wider. I became frustrated that I didn't have the skills I needed and couldn't grow as an artist.

After an unsuccessful job – a result of my lack of experience – the work dried up for a while, and so did my bank balance. My confidence took a knock, and I wondered if the world of make-up was really for me.

On top of this, I was single again. I decided I needed a break from London, a break from work and a break from the parties and boys. It was time to re-group and re-focus, so I packed up my make-up in my old kit bag and sought refuge in the safety of my family's wok.

I bid farewell to Donna, leaving the flat in Southfields that had been the scene of so much fun, and said thanks to Sally, explaining I needed some time out.

I went back to Leicester to lick my career wounds and make a decision – was it make-up or bust?

Dear Donna,

I'll always try to forget your horrendous bacon and cabbage! When I heard you'd passed away, I felt guilty that we'd lost touch. But then I remembered how much fun we'd had and realised that saying goodbye could never be as powerful as the memories we have.

RIP darling ...

CHAPTER NINETEEN

One of the IT Crowd

Giving up make-up was hard – I'd been given a taste of glamour and glimpsed a world I wanted to belong to – but this time going back home was not as difficult as it had been when I'd left Central. Then, anorexia had forced me back. This time I'd made the choice myself to return to the security of my family, where I could take some time out while I considered what I would do next. Now I saw home as a source of strength rather than as a place I went to when I failed. Going back would help me move on to the next experience of my life.

It was lovely to be home in many ways (I always enjoy being back in the comforting maternal embrace of Momma Wan), but over the next few months, I knew that Leicester wasn't where my heart was, just where my family was.

With fortuitous timing, my friend Phil called and said he was looking for a flatmate. Phil and I had been boyfriends for a brief week before we realised that our tongues were more suited to chatting than kissing, and we had become good friends.

Although I didn't have a job, I knew I had to seize this chance. I missed E'lain and my other friends, and the buzz of the Big Smoke. I was thankful that Leicester would always be home but I wouldn't be happy unless I was living in London, whether I was working in make-up or not.

I decided that it was irrelevant what job I did when I moved back – my first priority was to make some money. I didn't want to be living back in London, barely able to make ends meet, as that was partly what had caused my problems last time, and I was very aware this was my third attempt at making London my home. There was no room for mistakes.

I began to look for a job in London while I was still at Mum and Dad's, but I had no idea of what I wanted to do. Acting was a long-gone ambition and the make-up industry seemed too hard to break into.

I called a friend who was working as a recruitment consultant and asked her advice. She knew I had no formal qualifications and no real skills other than basic make-up and, to my complete amazement, she suggested I try recruitment. She told me the working days were long and that it was really only a sales job hidden behind a business card, but since I was good with people and I could talk the talk she believed I would be very good at it.

With her recommendation, I searched online and found a company advertising jobs for junior account managers in IT recruitment. The basic salary was poor but the advert tempted me with its promise of limitless earning potential. I had no IT skills, other than knowing how to surf the Internet, but the advert assured me full training would be given with no experience required.

I called, attended an interview and within two weeks I was back in London, starting work as a recruitment consultant. Was this it? Had I found my true vocation? Would recruitment consultancy be the lover I had always been searching for?

Was it bollocks! It was SHIT!

Phil and I found a house in Vauxhall and became roomies. The house was warm and loving and became my home away from Leicester. It was somewhere I finally felt safe and comforted. From the moment I walked in I knew it would be a special place. It's where I grew into the person I am today.

I started work in an agency near Tower Bridge, where the boss took great pleasure telling us all how much money she was making and what she was spending it on, which did nothing for morale. I was there for a couple of weeks before I could stand her tales of the high life no longer and walked out.

I managed to get another job in a company over the river near Spitalfields and stayed there about three months, before I joined my third (and final) IT recruitment company, staying there for about eight months. I don't know how I managed that long as I knew absolutely nothing about IT recruitment, but I was kept on as I was confident with customers. I'd sweet-talk them, charm them, take them out for lunch and drinks and make them laugh. I didn't do one deal the whole time, but the clients came back because of me, and others in the office dealt with the recruitment side of things. So I was worth a salary to the bosses, though it didn't make me anything at all beyond my miniscule basic as I never directly earned any commission.

I was skint and getting into debt again, and I was bored witless in an office job. Plus, sitting behind a desk all day meant that I gained two stone in weight over the year. The only thing that kept me going was being in London and the security of being close to my 'alo alo' friends, as I called them, in Vauxhall.

I was miserable and I couldn't believe I had failed again. Was this going to be the trend for the rest of my life? I'd wasted another fucking year of my life and I was back to square one, only more miserable and *fucking fat, AGAIN*!

After consulting with my friends and family, I made one of the best decisions of my life. I handed in my notice, burned my cheap Burton's suits and took a job as a waiter in a restaurant in Kensington.

*

After a year of achieving very little, it felt brilliant to work at something I knew I could do. I didn't care that my waiter's job didn't come with a business card and brief-case, I didn't care that I wasn't needed for team briefings or client meetings, and I didn't care that it looked as though I had slid backwards on the career ladder. Wait-ing was in my blood and I was fucking good at it.

I loved being in the restaurant, which was a predom-inantly gay establishment serving expensive pub-style food – fish and chips, bangers and mash, shepherd's pie – and I took to it with the ease of a duck paddling back into a familiar pond.

Within a couple of months I'd lost the two stone in weight and cleared off some of my debts with my hard-earned tips. I took great pleasure in making sure my diners had fun and were well looked after, and in return they tipped me handsomely. Just as I had done as a child in Dad's restaurant, I tried to work the tables with so much flare and enthusiasm that the customers would feel guilty if they didn't overspend. I quickly remembered how to assess whether a table would tip over a fiver, and those I thought looked promising would receive the special 'Gok treatment'.

Because of my Asian looks, the old boys would often request me as their server. I would undo an extra button on my shirt, sit on their knees when taking their orders and sometimes brush my hand over their shoulders when I delivered their bill. It was a sure-fire way to guarantee a

£20 note stuffed into my trouser pocket. On a good night I could take home up to £200 in tips. It may sound like I was a hooker in waiter's clothing but it was harmless – I did no more and no less than a shot girl in a vodka bar.

Working in the restaurant also gave me enough free time to work out what my next career move should be. During my time off, I would fantasise about where my life would take me in ten years' time. (Naturally I had no idea I would be sitting down to write my autobiography!) For a brief period I considered going back to drama school, this time a little wiser and stronger, but I knew I still hadn't fully recovered from my last attempt. I toyed with the idea of staying in catering, maybe moving into management, but I knew I would only get bored and end up having to start over again. So I decided I would give make-up and styling one more shot.

CHAPTER TWENTY

Agent X

When I'd worked with Sally Simpson, I had met other make-up artists, hairdressers and stylists and all of them had spoken about their agents. For 20 per cent of an artist's earnings, the agents would find work for them, negotiate deals, handle invoices, liaise with clients and generally make sure the artists were working for the right brands. I figured that if I was going to make it in the business, I needed to get representation. But I was also aware that I was inexperienced and that would make it hard to get an agent, and impossible to get one of the top ones, who would only take on very established artists. I had to get one, though, as I was sure I wouldn't get work without representation.

The fashion industry is notoriously snobby about who an artist is represented by. Top agencies in London only deal with the most prestigious clients and they only want hot-shot make-up artists on their books. I wasn't a hot-shot make-up artist but I knew if I could just convince an agent to put me on their books I could teach myself as much as I needed to know to go from cold shot to a sizzling one. One major obstacle was the fact that I'd never assembled a portfolio of work to show as evidence of my work, something that was absolutely vital. Without a portfolio, no agent would ever take me on. So I decided I would have to get creative.

I don't know if it was the confidence I had found from doing well in the restaurant that allowed me to make this leap of faith. Throughout my entire career, the best opportunities have always arisen when I'm feeling good about myself, whether it's landing a styling contract with a band, being asked to present on TV or being asked out on a date. You can guarantee it only ever happens when I am feeling good about Auntie Gok.

It was the early summer of 2000. I was twenty-six, still living in Vauxhall with Phil, and earning a decent amount at the restaurant. Life felt good and I sensed opportunities only just out of reach. I wanted to grab them.

One day, I sat myself in a café, just off Soho Square, armed with an *A to Z* and a pile of glossy magazines. I carefully went through each one and made a note of all the agencies that represented make-up artists who had work in the magazines. It seemed that Carol Hayes Management had had a good month as they were at the top of the list. I called right away and made an appointment to go in and introduce myself. They said I could come in an hour to talk to an agent, and gave me the address of the agency. I checked my map and luckily the agency was based just minutes away from the café. This was it!

An hour later I walked into their offices. Carol Hayes Management was based on the first floor of a purpose-built block. My first impression was that it was a bit grey and didn't look like a top agency; in fact it could have been any office. In all fairness, I had no idea what a top agency would look like, but there were no security guards, no posters of *Vogue* covers on the walls and Jerry Maguire was nowhere to be seen. Instead it was noisy: telephones were ringing, people were shouting and there was a constant stream of people walking in and out looking either fabulous and Sally Simpson-esque in drapy black layers, or dressed down and casual in jeans and sports tops.

All of them seemed to be carrying huge portfolio cases, which made me feel nervous and not a little bit sick. I realised that I was really taking a risk deciding to blag my way into a place like this, but dammit, I'd talked my way into and out of some situations in the past, surely I could pull this off as well? I tried to stay confident and calm.

I sat in reception and waited for my appointment with the agent who'd agreed to see me. My heart was racing. What the hell had I done? Surely whoever it was would see through my bullshit and kick my arse out the door the minute I opened my mouth.

After a short wait, I was called into the office to meet the agent, who introduced herself as Julie. She was a real stunner and I later found out that Julie had once been a model before becoming an agent and head booker for Carol Hayes, the boss of the agency.

I could see Julie was trying to work me out. She made no secret of assessing what I was wearing, and generally taking me in me from top to toe to see if I was a genuine article and right for the agency. My nerves began to take over, so I switched into automatic pilot. Just be charming and plausible, I told myself, and then you can get out of here without being kicked out. I introduced myself with a confident handshake and smiled warmly. We sat at the large desk and began to chat. I told her I had been a make-up artist for many years (blag) and I apologised for not having a portfolio to show her, as it was in New York with a film company (I'm blushing as I write this!). I explained I had done lots of work but I had represented myself (lots of work = lie; repping myself = true). I dropped a few names of photographers (all from the magazines I had just read) and then finished my pitch by telling her that I was a confident and competent artist who would be willing to do any job she threw at me.

Julie was very nice, thanked me for coming in and said she would be in touch if she thought that there was room for me on the books. There it was – all over in about twenty minutes. I left the agency with no idea of how it had gone. Had Julie seen through my web of lies or had I managed to woo her with my eager and enthusiastic smiles?

Amazingly, Julie called me the following day and told me that Carol Hayes Management would be happy to put me on their client list. I was overjoyed. I couldn't believe I'd been able to pull it off and get myself an agent at such a prestigious agency.

I later found out that Julie had sussed my inexperience right away but she had liked me and thought there was something about me that was refreshing. She saw past my bluster and gabbling and thought I would get on well with clients, so she decided to give me a chance.

I was so grateful for my new opportunity that I resolved I would work as hard as I possibly could for the agency and justify their faith in me. I went home, dusted off my make-up kit and prepared for the next move forward in my career.

A few days later I received a call from my new agent. Julie told me she had optioned me to do a job for *Cartier Magazine* and I would be grooming the British Polo team. What a fucking result!

I decided I needed a whole new look if I was going to be a successful make-up artist so I went shopping. I chose a skater boy image, with baggy combats, skater trainers, skater chains, hoodies and little caps. I wasn't yet wearing glasses, but if I had been you can bet they would have been skater boy ones. With my new outfit, I had that extra dash of confidence I needed to get by.

I went on the *Cartier* shoot, had the time of my life and the job went well. I was prepared to put my heart and soul into succeeding this time, and it felt for the first time as though everything was right. I knew how much was riding on this and I couldn't afford to turn away from it.

I also felt as though I'd found a home. The agency was on my side, and I was back in a world where I felt I belonged. I enjoyed being with photographers, models, stylists, fashion editors and people who worked in the industry. I had things in common with them. My personality fitted in here. I was around similar people, allowed to be silly and smoke and wear what I liked. There were few boundaries, and although we worked very hard and put all the hours we had into getting the right results, it was still relaxed. I thrived in a creative environment, and felt at home in a way I never would in an office.

Now I was prepared to put my head down, work, learn and become the success I'd always known I could be, if only the right chances came my way.

Dear Meneh,

You have shown me such great friendship since the day we met at Central. You are one of the few reasons why I do not regret my time there. You have tirelessly listened, cared and supported me, thank you. I love and care for you so very much and not a day goes by without my being grateful to have you in my world. I love you.

    Gok x

Tom Yum Facial

INGREDIENTS

Tom yum paste (or stock cube)
Bag of frozen mixed seafood

OPTIONAL

Two eggs
Fine egg noodles
Fine green beans

METHOD

This recipe serves two best friends. Add tom yum paste or a stock cube to two pints of water. Bring to the boil. Add a defrosted bag of mixed seafood (or just prawns, if preferred). This is now ready to eat as is (for those crazy weeknight catch-ups when time is at a premium) but you can also add the following ingredients to make the dish extra-special: two portions of fine egg noodles, a handful of chopped green beans and, finally, crack in two eggs for the 'King of One-bowl Meals'. Add a dash of white pepper just before serving as, baby, it can never be hot enough! Place in two large bowls. Eat using chopsticks and Chinese soup spoons (if you have them). Sit facing each other cross-legged on the floor and lean over for the world's best Tom Yum facial steam ever. Interrupt slurping only to catch up on the latest gossip.

Recipe by: Lainey V

CHAPTER TWENTY-ONE

The Label Says It All

O ver the next couple of years, I had the time of my life. The agency worked hard to get me out in the industry meeting magazine editors, art directors, casting directors and music video commissioners. I developed my make-up skills and even built a strong portfolio.

I also found the confidence to begin styling. I'd loved helping Sally and I knew I had a greater strength with clothes than with make-up. I seemed to understand clothes more. Make-up was fun and creative but at times its limitations bored me. Styling never did. I enjoyed the human contact that came with dressing a client. I loved making contacts with the PRs, the shopping was always exciting and convincing my clients what their new image should be was rewarding.

It was great to have two skills that were marketable in the same industry. The agency sold me as a make-up artist, but I was also able to keep the clients' fees down if they booked me for the styling, too (one hotel room, flight and evening meal – deal!). At the time, I was just about the only artist in London who offered this service, which meant I could monopolise the industry and keep a full diary.

Soon after joining Carol Hayes Management, I was out on a drunken night in Soho and I met a stock image library producer called Simon Ashley (soon to be nicknamed Big Bear). Big Bear worked as a freelance producer and ran a business with a photographer called David Leahy (aka Leaky Bottom). The two of them funded trips abroad shooting generic photo shoots that would be sold into image libraries that would, in turn, sell those photographs to the media to use illustratively. Not all images you see in the magazines are shot specifically for that story. Let's say you read a story about the burden of household debt and you see a photograph alongside the article of a couple sitting at a kitchen table looking worried as they study a bill. That picture probably came from an image library, which holds hundreds of thousands of photos available at a fraction of the price of what a photo shoot would cost.

Big Bear, Leaky Bottom and I became photographic Musketeers, travelling the globe and shooting story after story for the libraries. We could pitch up in Arizona for three weeks and after a couple of days of pre-production – casting models, scouting locations and, of course, prepping

Life as a make-up artist – the top three
taken while working on a film about Neo
Man (Glam!) and below at a wedding in
Spain where I was booked by Leaky
Bottom to do his mates' make-up

'Naked is what I do.
Been there, done that,
and ripped off the
t-shirt' – from series 2

In 2007 we won Best Lifestyle
Show at the TV Quick and
TV Choice Awards

Filming with my TV mum –
Ms L K herself. Just gorgeous!

© PA PHOTOS

Dynasty meets
the Ming Dynasty!

If We had kids
their surname
Would be Wan-Carr!

© ENDEMOL

Just
checking
Piers!!!

© JASON JOYCE

Interviewing
the *SATC* girls
at the film
premier, 2008

Carol Hayes
(my agent),
Charlie Duffy
(my make-up
artist) and a
team of
photographic
geniuses after
a photoshoot
for *GQ* mag

My goddaughter
Yasmina, on her
first birthday

My nieces Maya-Lily
and Lola-Rose

With my best friend E'lain

My parents meet Gordon
and Sarah Brown, at their
Chinese New Year tea party,
February 2010

Oilen and me –
I love this pic!!!!!!!

Best man at
Kwok-Lyn's wedding

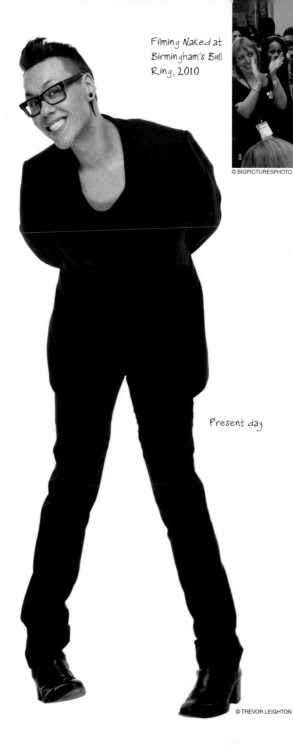

Filming *Naked* at Birmingham's Bull Ring, 2010

© BIGPICTURESPHOTO.COM: 1661

Present day

© TREVOR LEIGHTON

the clothes – we would begin shooting for two weeks. The days were exhausting but I learned so much about the job. Not only did I have to perform miracles with the hair and make-up (not all the models were professional; some were 'street castings', where we approached people who had the right look and asked them if they wanted to model). I would also have to source and style the clothes (often bought from local shops and then returned to save budgets) as well as 'style up' the locations with accessories and props.

We would very often shoot at least four stories in one day. A typical working day might begin by shooting a story about 'Love', using various couples eating, pillow fighting, walking hand in hand, eating out, kissing and so on. Then we'd move on to shoot a 'Beauty' story, this time with girls applying make-up or face products, bathing and receiving therapies. In the late afternoon, we'd shoot a story about 'Travel'. Our models would be packing luggage, waiting in airport terminals, booking flights, etc. We'd finish off the day with an evening shoot about 'Nights out' – girls drinking cocktails in a bar, dancing in a club, applying make-up in club toilets and so on.

On a single day's shoot we could take well over a hundred pictures and each one would need to look generic enough to sell to a commercial market, but still be glossy and aspirational. I was responsible for every element: clothes, props, hair and make-up, as well as some of the art direction. I learned which clothes looked right for any occasion, whether it was a full-length evening dress or casual wear for a beach picnic. And at last I had the freedom to experiment with make-up looks and styling, and try out more unusual looks and techniques, and this helped me to expand my repertoire in a way I hadn't been able to when I worked on magazine shoots.

After two weeks of this, we would all be utterly shattered. I would return from a trip exhausted and burned out, but my new love of image and style fed me so much adrenalin, I wanted more!

My work diary was booked up weeks in advance and I knew the agency was happy with the amount of work I was doing, and pleased clients were coming back to rebook me. I put all my stock image work through the agency, so I was bringing in money for them and showing them my talents. Carol Hayes, the boss of her eponymous agency, started to take some notice of me. She had built the agency up from scratch herself, turning it into one of the most respected in the country, and she was the kind of powerful, successful woman I have always admired and been drawn to.

In the early days I was far too unimportant to attract her notice and she had such a formidable reputation that I was a bit frightened of her. When we did meet, I put on my most confident act to impress her, with the result that she thought I was a bit of an obnoxious git who loved the sound of his own voice. But as she began to see how much work I was doing and how hard I applied myself, she began to warm to me. I was obviously doing something right and she respects anyone who puts their back into things. It wasn't just about being booked for jobs; it was having clients come back to me that was the key. Carol always maintained there was enough work to go around once but you'd never sustain a career in the industry unless you got re-booked – wise words that I kept close to my heart.

I confided to Carol that I'd always loved performing, had some stage training and would be keen to try television if that ever came my way. No one else at the agency worked in television, but occasionally Carol would get calls from television people who specifically required a stylist or make-up artist to perform on a show, and she said that if anything came up that seemed suitable for me, she would put me forward.

I didn't know if that would ever happen, but it was nice to dream that one day I might get a chance to let my inner performer out just a little more.

Dear Carol,

You are more than an agent, you are my friend. You have shown me so much support over the years and I need you to know I appreciate your constant guidance. I feel lucky to have you

represent me. You are brilliant, kind, genuine and
honest, as well as a good and generous person.
Never let me go.
  Gok x

Meanwhile, my work away from the image libraries was developing. I began to get castings with record labels asking me to style and do make-up on bands and singers for videos, press tours and personal appearances. These jobs were always slightly trickier, as I had to learn quickly how to deal with musician's egos, which were sometimes more precious than models'. The girls were there to work but the musicians often acted as though they were doing you a big favour. The 'talent' could change their minds three or four times before I did the job and more often than not it would happen a few hours before I was due on set to shoot the video. The budgets were so small, I would often have to customise very cheap clothing to make the talent (mentioning no names) feel he or she was wearing something unique that no one else could have.

On a few occasions, the talent insisted s/he would only wear designer clothes but the record label would take me to one side and tell me they didn't have the budget for that type of thing. Many of the designers wouldn't lend clothes to me, either, because the artist wasn't right for the brand or because there wasn't any way they could get a credit (credits are usually only ever given in magazine editorials on a fashion photo shoot specifically designed to show off the clothes).

Instead, I discovered a market stall in Shepherds Bush that sold designer tags – literally, the labels that are stitched into the back of clothes. They were such good copies, I bought every single one and, the night before the video shoot, I would cut the labels out of the customised M&S, Topshop and Hennes garments and replace them with Dolce and Gabbana, Prada and Armani tags. The talent didn't have a clue! I got complete satisfaction from foiling my label-loving clients. 'Darling, this has only just arrived from Paris so you can't keep or buy it, but you look *sensational*!' (Between you and me, that would not be Paris, France, but Paris, Primark.)

Life was great. For the first time in my life I was beginning to feel settled and focused. I was no longer worrying about my weight, acting seemed positively pedestrian compared to my new, glamorous life and I was growing into a competent, confident stylist and make-up artist.

I had a great home life living with friends and partying hard on my rare time off, and I was slowly beginning to build up a small amount of savings. My days of living in broken-windowed bedsits, scraping rent together and feeling like the world's fattest failure seemed like a lifetime away. My weight was stable and the anorexia was at bay. Not even the bad gigs got me down ...

One memorable job was a pure make-up gig. The agency called and told me I had been optioned to fly to the Czech Republic for a men's magazine shoot (not top shelf stuff but definitely riskier than *The Lady*!). I had done make-up for this type of magazine before and it was usually an easy, straightforward affair. The girls needed heavy eyes, fake lashes and bucket-loads of tinted body moisturiser – glamour models do love sheen!

The agency gave me all my travel details but not much more information than that. As I packed my kit, I made sure I had a good supply of fake lashes and enough clothes for five days. (Although I was only staying away for three nights, Mum had taught me always to be prepared.)

Due to the flight being delayed, I didn't arrive in Prague until nearly midnight, which meant I missed the fast train to Brno, where the job actually was. Exhausted and a little concerned, I travelled the circumference of the Czech Republic on a slow train accompanied by staring soldiers with rifles. At every stop the soldiers checked everyone's passport, including mine, obviously looking for fugitives. It was scary, to say the least, and not a safe place for a Chinky make-up artist.

I finally arrived in Brno at 4 a.m. to a deserted city. The grey Eastern Bloc architecture was far from welcoming but fortunately the hotel was opposite the train station. After such a shaky start, I had the grim feeling of inevitability – this job was not going to go smoothly.

After three hours' sleep, I ventured down to the breakfast room in search of the art director and photographer. The room looked like it had not been decorated in years. The tables were sparsely laid over plastic cloths, and most seats had been taken by travelling businessmen, all wearing grey suits and trousers that didn't quite hit their ankles.

As I entered the room, an old woman plodded over to me and asked if I wanted tea or coffee while pointing in the direction of the buffet (mmm, yum, you can imagine ...). I asked for coffee and told her I wasn't hungry. The lack of sleep and growing apprehension had stolen my appetite.

I sat for ten minutes, nursing my coffee, waiting to see if the crew might arrive, but they didn't. Glancing out of the window, I noticed six blacked-out Mercedes cars parked outside the hotel, each one with a driver standing next to it in a grey suit and black sunglasses. It looked like a scene out of *The Godfather*. I decided the drivers and cars must have something to do with the shoot, so took my bags and went to investigate. I walked up to one of the drivers and asked if he was with the magazine shoot. Without a word, he looked me up and down, dropped his roll-up on to the ground and motioned his hand towards the second car.

Being either brave or stupid, I obediently loaded my bags into the boot and sat myself down in the back of the car. I introduced myself as 'Gok, the make-up artist from London' to the driver and with a flick of his eyes in the rear-view mirror he acknowledged me, not saying a word. We sat in complete silence for about ten minutes until a gaggle of very slim, very blonde, very young girls walked out of the hotel and bundled themselves into the remaining cars.

We set off.

We drove out of the city and within moments I was surrounded by the beautiful Czech countryside. The fields were so green, they looked almost untouched by humans. With my tinted window wound down, I enjoyed the views for the hour-long ride until we arrived at a huge, newly-built house at the entrance to a meadow.

As the car stopped in the driveway, a woman with glasses and very plain clothes appeared on the steps to the entrance of the house. I got out of the car, thanked my driver (he didn't respond, of course) and walked up to her. I introduced myself and was relieved to find she could speak basic English, although with a strong accent.

'Nicing to meet you, Gork. Come zis vay.'

I followed her inside. The house was beautiful but it was obvious no one lived there, as it was quite bare of furniture or anything to make it homely.

'Iz zis table okay for you to be working on?" the woman asked, pointing to a trestle table in the centre of the room.

'Yes, that's fine, thanks,' I replied, and started getting my kit out. No sooner had I laid my brushes out, then I heard the clicking of cheap heels and I knew my models had arrived.

Like a scene from *Legally Blonde,* the girls walked in. None of them were over a size six, all had cheap blonde hair extensions that looked as if they'd been ripped out of Dolly Parton's head and they all had tracksuit bottoms rolled down just far enough for me to see their navel jewellery.

I went up to the woman I'd met earlier who seemed to be in charge. 'Can I speak to the photographer so I can ask him what he wants? Are we shooting inside or outside? Can I see the clothes so I can match the colours?'

'Ee iz busy zetting up ze lightings, please making ze girls looking sexing.'

It seemed that was all I was going to get, so without proper direction, I began to make up the girls. Only one of the models spoke English. As I applied her base, I asked her a few questions about her life and work as a model. Her name was Katrina and she'd been modelling since she was eighteen, but she was giving it up to become an actress – apparently she was too old to be a glamour model. She told me she had only ever done glamour modelling but that she didn't do 'pink'.

'Pink?' I asked.

'Yes ... I do not do pink but all the other girls do.'

I blotted her lips and she left the chair. I figured 'pink' must be a kind of drug – maybe that's what the Czech called ecstasy or cocaine – but I didn't push for an explanation, as she didn't seem to want to talk about it.

By the time I had finished making up the sixth girl, I decided I would try and find the photographer. I could hear voices coming from the roof terrace. I followed the clicking noise of the flashes and the loud voice directing the girls in a foreign language, which took me up a flight of stairs to the roof.

On the roof there were four or five men – what their jobs were, I couldn't tell – and a photographer squatting behind a camera. I looked to where the camera was pointing and there sat one of the girls I had recently made up, completely naked, straddling what looked like an old milking stool. As my eyes became used to the blinding sun, I realised what 'pink' was ...

CHAPTER TWENTY-TWO

Wrap-around Ambition

Some people might assume that my TV success was given to me on a pink satin pillow one night, but let me tell you, it wasn't. If a princess must kiss several frogs before she gets her prince, then I shagged the arse off a trailerful of toads to get mine!

During 2005 and 2006, Carol put me forward for any jobs that came in and I auditioned for television thirteen times before I got my first three minutes on the screen. In 2005, Susannah Constantine and Trinny Woodall had just left the BBC and their hugely popular show *What Not To Wear*, defecting to ITV. The BBC was looking for replacement presenters and they called Carol to ask if she had someone who was suitable to go in and audition.

Of course, I leaped at the chance. *What Not To Wear* had been a huge success, catapulting Trinny and

243

Susannah into mega-stardom. Their sartorial flair coupled with middle-class bossiness had paved the way for a new breed of fashion television.

Since the early eighties, *The Clothes Show* and its like had dominated the fashion airwaves with straight-forward magazine-style formats. Then Trinny and Susannah had burst on to British television screens in 2001, demanding to know why the women of the UK were so poorly dressed. Their show had a reality makeover format, with Trinny and Susannah taking their ladies firmly in hand, often seizing their 'tits' and telling them in ringing tones where they were going wrong. The success of *What Not To Wear* was immense, as it was fresh, different and had no competition. It won awards and BAFTA nominations and sold around the world, spawning books and celebrity spin-off shows. It had run for five successful series when the girls decided to go to the 'other side' and they were a tough act to follow. It was a daunting decision even to think about auditioning but I had very little to lose having a go.

In preparation for my television auditions, I'd changed my look from skater boy to something a little more sober, predominantly black suits. I'd had my crooked teeth straightened and, following a diagnosis of short sighted-ness, I also wore dark-framed glasses. I hoped I looked right for whatever television people wanted, but it was much harder styling myself than styling other people. (As a rule of thumb, hairdressers usually have awful hair and stylists look terrible – they're too busy thinking about how other people look!)

On the day of the audition I was shown into a meeting room at the BBC, White City. Once again, I was struck by how unglamorous it was. The office could have been any office, a call centre selling insurance – anything, but not TV! Wogan wasn't at the coffee machine, French and Saunders weren't loitering in the corridors and Michael Aspel wasn't in his corner office. Auntie Beeb had fed us a lie for years!

The room had been cleared and the chairs had been swept to the sides of the rooms. A small home video camera had been set up in the corner to face a single office chair. The researcher who had shown me in asked if I wanted a drink and told me that the producers had run over in a previous meeting. I said it was fine and asked for a glass of water. As she walked out, she asked me if I minded if they recorded the interview. I told her I didn't and sat down in the auditioning chair.

I waited for over twenty minutes before anyone arrived in the room. It was the longest wait of my life. This was such a huge opportunity. Trinny and Susannah were big stars and although I had a very different approach to fashion, I was still super-nervous at the thought of trying to fill their size-seven stillies!

Eventually the door swung open and in trotted three women and the researcher, who was holding a plastic cup filled with my water. The women introduced themselves as the producers of the show and two of them shook my hand. The executive producer did not.

The 'exec' was everything you'd expect a stereotypical TV producer to be. She had obviously listened carefully to the advice of her previous two presenters as, I seem to remember, she was wearing a loud and heavily patterned wrap dress. The neckline was plunging like an Olympic swimmer and it showcased her TV silhouette perfectly – I could image T&S thrusting it at her insisting it was the type of dress she must wear until her dying day!

The producers settled in their chairs and the researcher pressed the record button on the camera. As the exec began to interview me, I noticed how uncomfortable she made me feel. Her eyes looked everywhere but into mine and she delivered her questions in a robotic way, as though they were a script she'd read a thousand times. It was obvious she thought she had better things to do with her time than interview me. It didn't matter that I'd hauled my ass all the way across town and was feeling nervous and anxious. God forbid she should try and make me feel relaxed.

The interview went *something* like this:

Exec: If you saw a woman in the street and she looked terrible, what would you say to her?

Gok: Well … I wouldn't say anything unless she asked my advice.

Exec: (Pause.) What if she asked you for advice, what would you tell her?

Gok: Well, that would depend on what she looked like.

Exec: I've already told you, she looks terrible!

Gok: Erm … It's hard to say because she's not real and therefore I can't see what she's wearing. But I'd probably suggest she try something different …

Exec: LIKE WHAT?! Come on, Gok, I need you to be bitchier!

Gok: That's not really my style, I'm sorry. If you want me to be a stylist and advise on fashion, that's not a problem, but I can't be a bitch to someone just for the sake of it, especially when she's not REAL!

Exec: Have you not seen the show?

Gok: Yes, I have! And I don't think I am what you are looking for!

And with that, I walked out of the interview. I left the BBC feeling disheartened. Was I only going to succeed in television by pretending to be something I wasn't? And how dare the producer assume I was a bitch! I'm a gay man, I can bitch as hard as the rest of them, but I wasn't going to slag someone off just because a camera was pointing at me! For a brief moment I wondered if in real life Trinny and Susannah were ministering angels sent by God to care for the WI, and not hard-nosed TV gals. Maybe it was the exec who had corroded their purity with TV acid. But it was only for a brief moment.

*

The BBC went with Lisa Butcher and Mica Paris as the new presenters of *What Not To Wear* and although they pulled in a respectable audience, the show was brought to an end in 2007. Carol continued to send me on auditions with production companies, screenings with casting directors and meetings with TV networks. None of them was right. There was either a problem with budgets resulting in de-commissioning and the channel not making the programme after all, or I wasn't quite what they were looking for. And, in all fairness, I was terrible in most of my auditions. The nerves would get the better of me and I would begin to panic.

I had started to despair that I had any chance of a TV career. The constant knock-backs reminded me of being at Central and I began to feel I wasn't good enough to make it. I decided that perhaps it was too dangerous to try this path. If my dream of performing was brought back to life and I didn't make it, it might provoke the self-hatred I had for myself whenever I felt that I'd failed. It would be a disaster if I started to lose focus on my styling career; it might even re-awaken the anorexia that I'd been able to suppress over the last few years while things had been going well.

To try and combat the insecurity and fear of failure, I reminded myself that I had built up a great career in fashion and that was enough.

But the TV gods must have been smiling down on me. One day *GMTV* called Carol and asked her if she had anyone on her books who could do a three-minute slot on Lorraine Kelly's breakfast show the day after the BAFTAs. They were looking for someone who could talk about the dresses with Lorraine. Carol suggested me, and they booked me without an audition.

I was excited but also terrified.

On the morning of the show I was picked up at the crack of dawn. I hadn't slept a wink as nerves had climbed into bed with me and talked all night long, filling my head with anxiety. What if I froze on camera? What if I said 'Fuck' by mistake? What if I couldn't remember the names of the actresses or the designers they were wearing? It was a long, sleepless night ...

It was still pitch black when we pulled up outside the studios. I'd been told to dress in a suit to complement the feature we were talking about. I must have looked like I'd been out all night as I rolled into the stage door in my Topman tuxedo. I was greeted by a woman who turned out to be a runner on the show (someone who works backstage getting people where they need to be at the right time) and I was amazed by how glamorous and 'done' she looked, in full make-up and heels at 7.05 a.m. She showed me into the make-up room, where I had an obscene amount of slap put on my tired face. I must have looked exhausted!

After my make-up was done, I was briefed by a producer on the dresses they wanted to feature and at 8.21 a.m. I was mic'd up and sitting on the sofa next to

Lorraine. I was totally star-struck. Lorraine Kelly, the Scottish institution with whom I had had breakfast each morning since the eighties, was sitting next to me wearing a beaming smile. She leaned over and said reassuringly, 'You'll be fabulous, darling. Just relax and enjoy.'

I was absolutely bricking it. The lack of sleep and pressure were all too much and my mind began to go blank. As I looked down at the cue cards the producer had given me to remind me of the sequence, my nerves robbed me of my sight and I couldn't read what the producers had written. The room began to spin and I started to sweat like a horse. Lorraine must have seen this and she simply placed her hand on mine. It was as if she had magical powers: she vanquished my fear and bought me back into reality with a soft smile. Now I knew I could do it.

The interview was great and Lorraine was just wonderful. She asked all the right questions, seamlessly filling any gaps with an encouraging comment like: 'That's a gorgeous dress, isn't it, Gok?' She made my three minutes of airtime feel completely natural. I will always be indebted to Lorraine for helping me launch my TV career.

After that, I was often on *GMTV* (and still am – I totally love Lorraine, who has repaid the favour by appearing on my show as well); I appeared on *T4* discussing the fashion of *The O.C.*, and narrowly avoided a national scandal when I swore on the Richard and Judy show (I was trying to remind myself not to say naughty words on air, and without meaning to I actually said one out loud just as we were going live. Thank goodness no one noticed).

It was official! I had developed a serious taste for the camera. Although I was still inexperienced and got very nervous before going on, I had learned not to be afraid to speak on screen. I loved the immediacy of TV and enjoyed having one chance to get my information over. I learned to be succinct and precise and, after a few more attempts, I started to add some humour. I knew this was something I could be good at. I loved fashion and now I was being given the opportunity to combine it with an element of performance. It was like my dreams had all come true. I was aware I had a lot to learn and I was still on the bottom rung of the TV ladder, but that was all right. Give me more!

CHAPTER TWENTY-THREE

Naked

One early job I auditioned for was a daytime fashion show called *Clothes Swap* on Channel 4. I shot a 'taster tape' (a sort of audition show reel for newbies) but while the show was still in development, Channel 4 commissioned *Deal or No Deal*, which quickly filled all the available daytime slots. As a result, *Clothes Swap* was de-commissioned.

I was disappointed but this proved to be a blessing in disguise. The commissioning editor for daytime programming, Mark Downey, was impressed with what had become my natural and fun presence on camera and he didn't want the channel to lose me to another network. He passed my taster tape to the head of prime-time features, Sue Murphy.

As luck would have it, Sue had been working on a new show idea to be called 'Naked'. The series was going to be the first of its kind, dealing with the everyday inse-curities women of the UK face with their bodies and going up against the fashion industry body ideal. The concept was a bold move, even for Channel 4.

As soon as she saw my taster tape, Sue knew I was perfect to front the series. She told me later that, in all her years of programming, she had never experienced such a positive, natural, almost fatalistic match. I was the right person at exactly the right time – luckily for me.

Unbeknownst to Sue, I had also that year auditioned for a series called *Make Me a Grown Up*, also for Chan-nel 4, made by Maverick TV. The show was more of an educational programme, where a team, including a styl-ist, would make over young adults in preparation for the next stage of their lives. It had looked as though it might be the perfect opportunity for me to dip my toe into the waters of TV.

Maverick had called Carol's office and asked me to attend a screen test for the show. I had arrived at John Lewis on Oxford Street where I met Colette Foster, a producer with a super-successful career in TV, regarded as one of the greatest minds in British features tele-vision. Her CV boasted a string of hit shows such as *The Clothes Show, Ten Years Younger, Embarrassing Illnesses, Gardeners' World* and the *Chelsea Flower Show*. She brought with her a researcher who was to film me on a small home camera. I was nervous, of course, but thanks to my previous experiences, I was beginning to learn that the audition process was just the start of a long, arduous journey to the screen and the chances were high that whatever it was we were doing would never be made, so I was also a bit more relaxed than I might once have been. I had decided I would just do what I have always done – entertain.

Colette had arranged for me to meet and do a makeover for a woman called Lizzy in the women's clothes department of John Lewis. I was told Lizzy was on her lunch break from an office job – what I didn't know was that Lizzy was actually a 'plant' and, in fact, a researcher on the show.

'What would you do with Lizzy?' Colette asked. 'What cuts suit her shape? Is she dressing right for her age? Can you make her look more glamorous?'

This was easy! I had been dressing women for years and because Lizzy had arrived in casual clothes, it was simple enough to make her look dressy, sophisticated and sexy. As I dressed Lizzy, I asked her, 'What parts of your body do you not like and what parts of your body do you not want to show off?'

Lizzy replied, 'I hate my stomach, I have a muffin top and I can't seem to find jeans that fit!'

And then it happened.

'Lizzy, you're cute, young, slim and pretty. You have a perfect shape and just because you are conscious of your tummy, it doesn't mean you shouldn't show it off. You just need to find clothes that will make you feel confident, and forget about the parts of your body you don't like.'

I had no idea I had just set the tone for my future television career. Where others bullied and commanded, I was about building up people's confidence and making them feel comfortable in their own skin.

Colette seemed pleased with the audition and *Make Me a Grown Up* went into production. I wouldn't get much airtime on the show but it was enough to learn a bit about how to work on camera.

While I was filming *Make Me a Grown Up*, Sue Murphy had instructed Maverick TV to begin developing the 'Naked' idea and told them she had seen the taster tape of a new talent called Gok Wan, and she thought I should present the show. Maverick was overjoyed, as they had already started to build a working relationship with me. Fate had brought us all together and within a month, production on the first series of *How To Look Good Naked* had begun.

It was amazingly exciting. I'd landed the dream job, presenting my own show. Of course, we had no idea whether it was going to be successful but it was still going to be an incredible experience. TV didn't pay as well as styling, unfortunately, and it would be very hard work, but I didn't mind. I knew this was my big break.

Pre-production started in the spring of 2006. Maverick TV employed a bright and ambitious production crew, including some of the most respected features TV makers the country had to offer.

I was called into Maverick HQ for bonding sessions with the team and I was amazed at their dedication to the job. I'd worked with many great fashion industry professionals but I had never met a more hardworking, ambitious and can-do team. The success of a series is hugely dependent on the crew and their devotion to the show, and our crew was second to none. They gave all their time, knowledge and passion for the duration of the production. Not only did they have a wealth of knowledge about what we were doing, but the budget was so tight that most of the team would have to work extra hours, weekends and be away from home without any extra money. They were all prepared to do that without complaint.

Colette Foster was in charge and during the pre-production meetings, her vision for the series jumped from the pages of her notepad and into the minds of her producers at a rate so fast it made my head spin. The room was full of imaginative energy, so much so that I sometimes felt as though I was standing in a wind tunnel, being buffeted with the force of everyone's creative powers. I would sit and watch Colette discuss, argue, convince and dictate the format of the show to her dutiful team. She knew what she wanted and made them go and get it!

I developed a great deal of respect for the production team and I made a pact with myself that I would never turn into a diva, demanding special attention because I was the talent. I vowed never to belittle or patronise the team because I was the face of the brand. I also promised myself that if I would never get my head stuck up my ass and treat any of the team like staff – as I had sometimes been treated when I was a stylist. I made that promise and to this day I have never broken it.

It was drawing closer to our first day of filming. Because TV was still virtually a new experience for me, I didn't feel the same anxiety as the rest of the crew in the lead-up to filming. I had no concept of the size of the risk it was to make a show like *How To Look Good Naked*. I didn't worry that a huge amount of money was being spent on a new TV show with an optimistic ethos, a cutting-edge approach and a lot of naked bodies to be shown before watershed. In among all the stress and panic, I simply attended the meetings and enjoyed getting to know the team.

The format we developed was straightforward. The show aimed to debunk body-fascist myths of perfection perpetuated by the fashion, beauty and advertising industries. Our mantra was 'Size hero, not size zero' and the programme was about helping women re-build their confidence and be happy with the way they were. There was no need to go on punishing diets or have cosmetic surgery – every woman was beautiful in her own way, with or without clothes. I would meet a woman who was very unhappy with the way she looked, to the point where it was inhibiting her life. Most were dressing in camouflage outfits of jeans and baggy sweatshirts, thinking this would conceal what they most disliked about their bodies. I would ask her to strip down to her underwear in front of three mirrors and talk frankly about how she felt about her body. At the same time, an enormous poster of our lady in her undies was displayed to the public and I would canvas opinions about her body from passersby, the better to convince her that she was seeing herself through distorted eyes. Then we would set about learning how to dress for her shape – the way underwear could help and what looks worked best – before giving her an all-over transformation that culminated in my asking her to pose naked for our photographer. It would be a long journey but, we hoped, an entirely positive one.

While the channel, producers, directors, crew and, of course, Colette could foresee the success of the show, I was blissfully unaware of how big it was going to be. If I had known I was about to be spring-boarded from anonymity into the public eye so fast I'd lose my under-wear, I think I might have run in the opposite direction. There was no way anyone could have prepared me for what was about to happen.

On the first day of filming my director Jenny said to me, 'Your life's about to change forever.' I giggled and tried to brush off what she had said, thinking she was just being polite. Of course, Jenny wasn't being kind or flattering me – she was, in fact, warning me! I've never forgotten those words and how right she was. I will always be indebted to her for the many words of wisdom she shared with me as we worked together.

Our first day of filming *How To Look Good Naked* tattooed itself on to my brain, and it was the last time I ever doubted that I wanted a career in television.

The soon-to-be famous nine-foot-high mirrors had been placed in the centre of the studio. The enormous camera lights had been erected on tall stands, every wire and lead had been carefully hidden under white gaffer tape, and the cameraman had set up his 'dolly' track that would allow the camera to move silently along the width of the studio.

Before we started filming, Colette, Jenny and I sat on a large leather sofa in the corner of the studio and mapped out the day's filming. They told me what they wanted to achieve while constantly reassuring me that I'd be brilliant, doing all they could to keep me natural and in control. They both knew that, as a complete novice, I was a huge risk to the production. I was a presenting virgin and if I froze on camera, or became awkward and stilted or, worse still, 'motored down tangent highway', then the day's filming would go up in smoke.

The sequence we were about to film was the opening to the show. Three mirrors would surround my lady and after I had asked why she had applied for help, I would invite her to strip down to her underwear and tell me what she thought of her half-naked reflection.

We had no idea what she might say. It was the first show and the mirrors were unknown territory. It was entirely possible that she might decide that she actually didn't hate her body as much as she thought! She might break down and run from the studio, sobbing at the humiliation we were putting her through. She might do anything! But the production team was fairly certain that we could predict the outcome – she would be honest and say she needed my help.

What no one had thought to predict was how I would react to my lady. At this stage, neither Colette nor Jenny knew that I had a history of obesity, self-abuse, crumbled self-esteem and body hatred. They knew that I was a fashion stylist capable of dressing almost anyone, and they'd seen from my taster tapes that I had a warm empathetic style, but that was as far as anyone had got with me.

And so the moment came. With the cameras rolling, I stood in front of the mirror with my lady and asked her to strip down, I saw the fear and embarrassment in her eyes. She tensed and tears sprang to her eyes, and I could see the struggle inside her. She agreed to do it, though, and, as she broke down in front of her reflection and told me that she hated her body, her pain hit me hard. I knew exactly how she was feeling. I put my arms round her, feeling every part of her anguish and fear inside me just as my own had been ten years before. I was taken back to the most difficult and awful time of life in an instant – I was reliving the pain I'd tried so hard to forget.

It was a long and hard day on set. We filmed two mirror sequences with my first two ladies. I was shocked at how much the women got inside my brain. I hadn't prepared myself to deal with the instant emotional attachment I felt towards my girls. I wanted desperately to speak to Colette and let her know I had been through a similar situation with my own body hatred but I was afraid she might think I was trying to upstage the women or even decide that I was too weak for the job, so I thought it was best if I dealt with it on my own.

Everyone was pleased with the first day's filming, but it was just the beginning, and until we got to the end of filming and constructed the programmes in the edit suite, no one would know whether it had worked or not.

The production ran for nearly three months. Every day on set was like my first day at school. It was enormously hard work. If there's anyone who thinks that working in TV is all relaxing cappuccinos and clocking off early, I can disabuse them of that. Working hours can be hideously long, and it wasn't unusual to clock up sixteen-hour days. But I had so much to learn and I loved it; I felt needed and important.

We made eight half-hour shows. Each episode featured a remarkable woman with a heart-stopping story. I fell in love with every single one of my girls, so much so that I felt incredibly responsible for them. What if I couldn't help them? They had nowhere to go if I closed my door on them. It was almost a paternal feeling. I knew that everything I said to them had a huge knock-on effect – they were relying on me and I couldn't let them down.

Towards the end of the production, as I gave the girls back to their families one by one, looking amazing and feeling better about themselves, each time it felt like an enormous weight had been lifted off my shoulders. I knew I had done the best I could to make them see how beautiful they were, and now it was up to them to maintain their new-found self-confidence. But I did miss them.

What I hadn't realised was that I had given so much of my heart to my girls, I was starting to crumble inside. I was exhausted. I hadn't slept properly for three months, as I would lie awake at night worrying about their future. The tiredness was starting to play tricks with my mind and I caught myself several times intentionally not eating, trying to gain some control in my life.

I was beginning to get skinny and gaunt and when I looked in the mirror I could see that my body and face were disintegrating. But I knew that it wasn't exhaustion that was causing my weight loss. I was racked with guilt. How could I stand in front of the camera and preach my new gospel of 'Size hero, not size zero' when all along I was pushing myself to the point of starvation? How dare I? What a fucking hypocrite!

In my defence, I did truly believe the women were beautiful; I loved their curves and bumps and I honestly did not think that they needed to lose weight to be gorgeous. I knew the mantra I was preaching to the nation was right, any success I'd had was always due to confidence, never to do with my size. But my illness was stronger than I was. My weight loss was not about being slimmer, it was about being in control. I needed time to feel at ease with what I was doing and to build up my confidence that I could do it. Then perhaps I'd be able to conquer my insidious enemy once more.

We were still in production when the first episode aired. It was broadcast at 8.30 p.m. and opened with me standing outside, my dark hair with a long fringe, wearing a pair of statement white-framed square specs. I spoke straight to camera. 'Do you avoid getting naked in front of the mirror?' I asked. 'Do you get undressed in the dark? Do you spend hours finding the perfect pair of jeans to stop your bum looking like a sack of spuds? Well, don't despair, and don't you dare go under the knife, 'cos I'm here to show you how to look good with your clothes on ...' – saucy little smile here – 'and off ...'

With that we were away, as I showed the lovely Susan from Yorkshire how she could stop hating her body and start cherishing her curves. It was an amazing transformation as she found her mojo again and realised that she was a truly beautiful woman. When we projected her glamorous naked image on to a London building to the universal appreciation of onlookers – including her husband – it was a triumphant moment.

While this was beaming on to television screens throughout Britain, I was still at work. It was a boiling hot day on the Embankment in central London and we were filming the final 'catch-up' with my last lady, in a beautiful riverboat restaurant. But as soon as the programme started to air, my mobile phone began to go crazy. I got texts from my family, friends, old friends I hadn't seen for years and, of course, Channel 4. Everyone was delighted with the show. I felt so proud of what we had achieved but the experience was so alien to me, it felt more surreal than celebratory. I was pleased our hard work had paid off. The hours of worrying, crying and not sleeping seemed a lifetime away and I just felt a huge sense of relief. But I also knew that might be short-lived, as the next day we would hear what the critics thought of the show, and find out the all-important viewing figures.

The following morning I bought every single tabloid and broadsheet. The press had gone crazy for the show. TV critics up and down the country had watched, scrutinised and made their decision. Most of the reviews were great, and praised our courage and vision. It felt good to be appreciated but the handful of bad reviews affected me more than I could ever have anticipated. Every bad write-up cancelled out the good ones and I felt as if everyone hated me. The critics obviously didn't have a problem with the ethos of the show; it was me they couldn't get their heads around, asking 'where on earth do they find TV presenters nowadays?'

The cruel words hurt so badly, it felt like every single letter was being hot-ironed on to my skin. I desperately wanted the journalists to like me and I didn't want them to poison the minds of the viewers against me. By mid-morning, I was in emotional turmoil, feeling as though, after all these years, a new set of name-callers had just been allowed into my life. Some of the press were viciously unkind, particularly about my looks. I was still so vulnerable to criticism after everything I'd been through.

I tried to tell myself I was a good person who was just trying to make a difference but the fat boy who still lived inside me wouldn't listen. It felt so unfair the press could judge me on how I looked. Had they not seen the show? It was all about accepting people for who they were and not what they looked like! Yet, I was now being told I was too weird-looking to be on TV.

Carol, Channel 4 and my producers tried to console me by telling me it was just part of the job but I didn't believe them (oh, the naivety!). I told them I wasn't being paid to be slagged off – but no matter how much I argued or got upset, the reviews didn't go away.

My other great fear was how my family would deal with the negative reviews. One tabloid wrote: 'Lisa from *Big Brother* [a Chinese contestant] is no longer the most annoying Chinese person on British TV.' I was so angry when I read this. How dare they be so racist? What did my race have to do with it? And I knew my dad bought that paper. I was scared I didn't have the power to protect my family. I had chosen this new career and they hadn't, but I had made them vulnerable to the media.

As the rest of the series aired, I found myself hiding in my flat. I didn't want to go out in case people hissed at me, laughed or, worse still, confronted me. I was so panicked that I called Carol and told her that I felt exposed. The entire country was talking about me and the show, and I was worried everyone hated me. My paranoia had grown out of control again.

Carol was great. She told me this was fantastic experience. I had to realise that I could never please everyone and inevitably there would be some people who didn't like it. But there were also those who just needed some time to get to know me and the show. 'The press needs something to write about,' she said wisely, 'and this week it's you. Readers like and need a variety of opinions but in the end they'll make up their own minds. It's the journalists who will get you well known, whether or not they like you, so try and relax and enjoy the ride.'

I would have been a great deal less frightened of the press if I could have seen into the future and had a glimpse of what our programme would achieve. None of us working on it had a clue that *How To Look Good Naked* was going to be one of the most recognised shows in the world, broadcast in over fifty countries, taking us into hundreds of millions of homes. We had no idea that in five years' time, degree students could choose to write their media studies dissertations on the format of the show. We didn't have the foggiest that over the next few years, we would put plus-sized models in mainstream ad campaigns and disabled models in the windows of one of the largest UK high-street stores, or that we would petition the government for, and win, a policy to get body confidence taught in schools. The phenomenon had already started, but all I knew was that there was a big, scary world out there.

But armed with Carol's words of wisdom, I put on my coat and went out there to face it.

Potato Latkes

INGREDIENTS

3 large potatoes, peeled and shredded
1 small onion, shredded
3 eggs
1 teaspoon salt
2 tablespoons all-purpose flour, or as needed
½ cup vegetable oil

METHOD

Place the potatoes and onion into a bowl, and stir in eggs, salt and flour as needed to make the mixture hold together. With wet hands, scoop up about ⅓ cup of the mixture per patty, and form into flat round or oval shapes.

Heat the vegetable oil in a large skillet over medium heat until it shimmers, and gently place the patties into the hot oil. Fry until the bottoms are golden brown and crisp, 5 to 8 minutes, then flip with a spatula and fry the other side until golden. Line a colander or strainer with two paper towels, and drain the cooked latkes in the colander. Serve hot and charge 20 per cent.

Recipe by: Dolly Dealer, aka Carol Hayes

CHAPTER TWENTY-FOUR

Never Ever...

Within days I began to feel better about the reviews. I was experiencing what the phrase 'tomorrow's chip paper' refers to. No sooner had the reviews been printed, the journalists were digging their pens, opinions and knives into the next poor sod. As cruel as it may sound, I was relieved it wasn't me!

Life slowly went back to normal. I began to eat properly again, I didn't have so many sleepless nights and I began to look forward to doing some more styling work.

Just after the series had finished airing, Carol received a call from EMI music. The head of A & R told Carol that the girl group All Saints had reformed and they were interested in hiring me as their stylist. The girls had seen *Naked* and they wanted to meet me. WOW! I couldn't believe the programme had worked as a PR drive and that even celebrities had tuned in to watch the show. What a head-fuck! Did this mean that perhaps even the Queen might have settled down with a microwave dinner on Tuesday nights and watched my show? Wicked!

Channel 4 hadn't decided whether they were going to re-commission the show so the All Saints job came at just the right time. The band had signed a one single and one album deal and had a ruthless press schedule ahead of them. They needed a stylist who could re-brand them and give them a new look for the video, press shots, interviews and CD covers. What a touch!

I was nervous as I entered the recording studio in Primrose Hill for my meeting with the girls. All Saints had been a huge band in the nineties and had made famous their casual look of combats and vest tops – I had certainly emulated their look on more than one occasion.

I had spent a few days researching and preparing what I envisioned for their new style. I knew I had to keep them looking 'poppy', but they had also grown up and had children. There was no way they could be slung back into combats and ponytails. They needed a new, sexier look that was casual enough for a back reference but was more of the moment.

I decided I would give the girls a 'sexy skater' image; that way, I could keep the casual image they were famous for. I would replace the combats and sneakers with skinny jeans and high heels but keep the sweatshirts, hoodies and urban sport-lux jackets. It would be a perfect mix of Gwen Stefani meets Avril Lavigne.

As I stood in the studio reception, a flash of confidence soared through me. Why was I so worried? They'd called me! If they didn't like what I had in mind for their new style, then I would simply turn round and go after the next job.

I realised then that *How To Look Good Naked* had given me a back-up plan; I had a second string to my bow, now, and I was no longer entirely reliant on my styling career for money or success because there was the possibility of a new career as a TV presenter. But just in case that didn't happen, I did still have my stylist work.

Feeling strong, powerful and confident, I was shown into the studio where the girls were laying down a track. As the door opened to a darkened studio, I got my first glimpse of the girls in the flesh. Instantly, my new-found confidence drained out of my body. Fucking hell, I thought. It's All Saints!

Nicole and Nat were sitting behind the mixing desk, Mel was perched at their side and Shaznay was standing behind them. The girls all looked towards me and in perfect harmony they said, 'Hi, Gok!' It was like I had gate crashed the set of *Charlie's Angels*.

'Hi,' I replied shyly as I walked through the doorway. I was so transfixed by the girls, I hadn't noticed there was a small step leading into the studio. I tripped down the step, lost my balance, fell through the door, stumbled forward two or three paces, throwing both arms into the air, and finally landed face down on the mixing desk.

It was truly the most humiliating moment of my life.

The girls screamed with a mixture of excitement and embarrassment and then fell about the studio in fits of laughter, clapping their hands together gleefully. I couldn't believe it. Sore faced and panicked, I tried quickly to regain my composure, pulling myself up from the desk but knocked backwards into a swivel chair, which threw off my balance once again. I must have looked like a six-foot, red-faced Chinese Frank Spencer!

After finding my feet, I apologised for my clumsiness. The girls were still laughing as they told me it was fine and asked if I was okay.

I told them I was, but I was lying. My pride had been seriously wounded in the fall and I wanted to run from the studio, find a quiet corner, curl up and die. Never, ever have I felt so ridiculous.(Recently Mel told me that they knew they were going to hire me the moment I fell over. 'It proved you were one of us,' she said.)

Once I'd re-gained my equilibrium, I raced through my ideas for their new style. The girls seemed to like the looks I'd come up with but I hardly noticed. I couldn't wait to get out of the studio.

A few hours after I'd managed to escape, Carol received a call from the girls' management telling her All Saints were very happy with me and I was booked. It looked as though the girls had fallen for me as hard as I had in front of them.

*

One of the first jobs we did together was the girl's come-back video, 'Rock Steady'. I had several meetings with the director, label, management and, of course, the girls. The story of the video was a 1920s, Bonnie-and-Clyde-style bank robbery with the girls pulling off a heist. Thankfully, I came up with an idea they all loved. I designed some vintage-looking costumes inspired from the thirties, forties and fifties and had them made in black-and-white PVC. It was rather like a bondage tribute to *Breakfast at Tiffany's*! The concept worked and the video looked amazing, very glam and stylish. The girls loved their sexy new image.

After the single was released, we went on a press tour around Europe. The girls had been booked on to all the breakfast, chat and music shows. They needed a different outfit for every appearance and I was the person responsible for making sure they always looked perfect, never duplicated a look and, more importantly, felt great in their clothes.

I decided it was better to take the girls shopping with me to fit them for their press tour outfits, as that way the girls could give me input into what they wanted to wear. I figured it would be easier to take the girls two at a time, so Mel and Nic went first. Naturally, all of the shops wanted the girls to be dressed in their clothes, so we were treated to five-star service with a team of personal shoppers on hand, and a couple of bottles of champagne on ice. Now that's what I call shopping!

In one shop, we were going through the rails of clothes and out of nowhere a gaggle of screaming and giggling teenagers came running up to us. Assuming the teenagers wanted autographs and pictures with the girls, I stood to one side but to my amazement, and Mel and Nic's shock, the group of teenagers rushed towards me and asked me for MY autograph! The look on Mel and Nic's faces was priceless. I blushed, gave the kids my signature and saw them on their way, then turned to Mel and Nic, grinned and said, 'Come on, girls, we've got eight outfits to find today, keep looking!'

With that, we all burst out laughing.

I loved working with the girls. We had our differences and sometimes it would result in fashion blows, but on the whole, it was great fun. I loved the dynamics of the band: Shaznay was the quietest of the girls but always in control; Mel and Nicole had re-kindled their childlike friendship and were always up to mischief; while Nat remained focused and determined.

All Saints were in demand and everyone wanted to interview them. The press were on the hunt for a scoop and sniffed about for gossip on why the band had origi-nally split in the nineties, but the girls had been brilliantly trained to bat away any intrusive questions. I watched and learned a lot about how to handle the press when they were in full bloodhound mode.

The first single 'Rock Steady' did very well and peaked

at a very healthy number 3 in the UK charts. The girls were overjoyed but they knew they had a long way to go before they had the same level of success as they'd had before. I was proud to be a part of their comeback.

Meanwhile, Channel 4 and Maverick were also working hard re-developing *How To Look Good Naked*. Although I didn't yet know it, Sue Murphy had re-commissioned the series and had decided to make it an hour-long show.

When Carol called to tell me they wanted me to film the second series, I couldn't believe it. I had slipped easily back into the familiar world of styling where I'd felt safe and secure, and I'd assumed *How To Look Good Naked* had been canned after one series. I wasn't aware the show had done surprisingly well, clocking up viewing figures of over three million households per episode. *Naked* was a huge success and was set to return in the spring of 2007!

It was brilliant news and I was hugely excited. I'd felt sure we'd done some amazing, groundbreaking telly that was able to touch hearts and change minds, and Channel 4 obviously thought so, too.

Fuck, though ... What about All Saints?

I spent days panicking about how I was going to tell the girls I was leaving. I was worried they would think me a traitor and a user. Would they think I had just taken the contract with them while I was waiting for something better to come along?

Although the band had employed me as a freelancer and I had the option to leave whenever I wanted to, I didn't want to let the girls down. For a brief moment I contemplated filming the new series as well as styling the band, but I knew it would be too much. I even contemplated not filming the show and staying with the girls, but there was no way I could turn down this opportunity. I had had a fabulous time working with All Saints but deep down, I knew that I was no longer happy simply being a stylist. I'd had a taste of the limelight I'd always yearned for and in the five months I'd spent with the band, I'd missed performing for the camera. Although there were aspects of presenting I didn't like – the media attention, the really long hours – I was hooked.

My greatest fear was that TV work would cause an onset of my anorexia; it had certainly affected me badly during the first series. But I'd had a few months out now to think it over and to understand why the disease had come back. It was because I'd felt out of control. Added to this, the show had made me re-visit my body hatred vicariously through the contributors; I was made to question what *I* thought when *I* looked in the mirror. I knew if I was ever going to make peace with my anorexia then I needed to *not* run away from what scared me.

All Saints took my departure really well – so well, I could have been slightly insulted if they weren't so lovely. In the lead-up to Christmas 2006, I told them I was leaving and with lots of kisses and promises to keep in touch, we said our goodbyes.

We began filming *How To Look Good Naked*, series two, in January 2007. I had decided I was going to make this series bigger and better. There was no way I was going to let the press beat me down: I was stronger. I knew I'd finally found the career I wanted to pursue and I was prepared to give it everything I had.

I wanted to learn everything there was to know about making a TV show. I wanted a say in the editorial decisions and I wanted the country to know that this show was about to change the shape of British fashion. The show's message was to become my personal vendetta against all those bastards who'd told me I was not good enough. I was going to prove to them I had been a good person when I was fat and I was the same good person now that I was thin. If anyone ever told me again I was not good enough, then I was prepared to fight them, bare knuckled, alongside my new naked army.

I was duly empowered and firing on all cylinders, but I began to notice that filming series two was different from series one, mainly because the women that had been cast on the show had watched the first series and knew what to expect.

The format of the show is built on surprises and without shock tactics we would never be able to get big genuine reactions from the ladies. To combat this, the producers decided they wanted to introduce a new finale: a catwalk for the ladies in nothing but their underwear.

I was worried this was too much for the girls. What if they said no? What if we got complaints from the viewers saying we'd pushed it too far? What if the press thought it was gratuitous and blamed me for it? Fuck!

I raised my concerns with the producers but they reassured me the ladies would be protected and we would never allow them to come to any harm, and I trusted what they told me because I'd seen how they'd looked after the ladies in the first series. Their naked photo shoots were carefully managed so that the women felt comfortable throughout and nothing was shown that would have embarrassed or offended anyone. I knew that the naked catwalks would be handled in the same way. The show's fashion producer, Jane Galpin, was hugely responsible for making sure the girls were cared for without compromise. Jane quickly became the show's conscience.

Once filming was underway, I fell in love with the show again. I slept well at night knowing *Naked* was an important TV show with a vital message of the zeitgeist, and I disagreed with the journalists who thought it was rude and inappropriate. I knew we were making a difference and challenging the fact that the fashion industry had, for a long time, been both elitist and promoted an unhealthy ideal of the female shape. For far too long women had been told they had to undergo masses of cosmetic surgery or they wouldn't be beautiful. What a load of old shit! Series one had already proved that with reassurance, guidance, some decent underwear and some well-chosen clothes, a woman could feel a hundred times better about herself. You didn't have to be a supermodel (i.e. impossibly thin and weird-looking in real life), or a beautiful actress (carefully shot in a professionally lit studio with the help of a make-up artist, hairdresser, stylist and our friend-the-airbrush), or a teenage beachbabe, to be a gorgeous woman proud of her natural assets.

Series one had been our pilot series and it had proved a hit; the second series was now going to be an hour-long show and Channel 4 was going to invest a lot more money in what would be a big, prime-time programme.

When we were making the first series, I'd sometimes been alarmed at the amount of emotion the ladies were revealing. Once or twice, I'd panicked and felt we were going beyond what a television show about getting some nice new clothes and a burst of confidence should attempt. But once the shows had been edited together and we'd seen them, it was clear that *Naked* was about much more than some new dresses. At its heart was the emotional journey the women were going on and the results of this journey for the ladies proved it was all worthwhile.

In series two, therefore, we decided to go deeper, really getting to know our ladies, their lives and their body hang-ups. Not all of our girls were curvy, either.

There were plenty of smaller-figured women out there covering up because they were convinced they were hideous. The show was creating a community, helping people to understand that they were not alone when they hated their bodies and felt dowdy and worthless.

There were some other format changes, too. Now the women came with me when I displayed their underwear shot at the start of the programme – resulting in some quick sprints for me as they ran away from it! We tackled issues like how to deal with body hair, tans and other treatments, and what lingerie suited which body shape. We had huge consumer tests, with a hundred ladies trying out the promises of different lotions and potions. We looked inside the girls' underwear drawers and I threw ancient, greying pairs of pants out of windows or on to burning braziers, urging them to find knickers that fit and flattered.

And, of course, we had our catwalk. It came as a shock to the ladies when I broke the news to them that I wanted them to model in front of thousands, ending up in only their underwear. Everyone could read the fear and apprehension on their faces, but they all gathered together their courage and did it, and I was amazingly proud of my brave girls. That moment – as my lady strode down the catwalk to cheers and applause (and maybe some tears) from her proud family and friends.

When the series aired, the viewers found it as moving and happy as I did. In fact, series two was to be a huge success and my life would turn yet another corner.

CHAPTER TWENTY-FIVE

The Big Time

The next six months were insane! The second series of *How To Look Good Naked* became one of the most talked-about TV shows in the country: we must have garnered more column inches than a Katie Price wedding! The newspapers and magazines loved it, the online bloggers loved it; even some of the critics who had doubted the first series were now backpedalling and praising the programme.

Carol's telephone was ringing off the hook. Offers seemed to come flooding in from every direction. Clients wanted me to open shopping centres, speak at charity shows, attend premieres and endorse washing machines, hair products, glasses, clothes and underwear. Carol and I would joke together that there wasn't a part of my body that couldn't sell a product. I trusted her judgement in the things that we chose to do: she advised me on what I should accept and what wasn't right for me. We remained selective about the clients we chose to work with, as we didn't want to sell out to the industry and I wanted to retain my integrity. I became a spokesman for SpecSavers, who sponsored the show, and wrote a book to tie in with the programme, also called *How To Look Good Naked.*

It wasn't just the commercial market that wanted to speak to us. Paul O'Grady wanted me on his sofa, Gordon Ramsay wanted me in his kitchen and even the prime minister wanted me in his home. I couldn't believe it. The fat, bullied kid from Leicester was now one of the most wanted boys in the country – how fabulous!

Along with all the excitement of success and the buzz of feeling wanted, I realised that my fame had hit a level no one could have expected. I would get stopped anywhere and everywhere I went and be asked for my autograph, a photo and, in many cases, advice. 'What dress shape am I?' women would ask. 'I'm going to a party on Saturday, what do you think I should wear?'

It felt like the country had taken ownership of the show. *How To Look Good Naked* was about real people *for* real people, so everyone felt they had a piece of it. In many ways I agreed with them – it *was* their show! We couldn't do it without our wonderful ladies, their friends and families and the members of the public whose opinions we canvassed or who attended the catwalk shows.

I think that my accessibility came from the fact that I didn't put on a performance that turned me into a different person – I was simply myself. In theory this was a good idea, but in reality it had its drawbacks. For one thing, everyone who had seen the show felt as if they knew me. I loved meeting fans and talking to them. I didn't say no to autographs and pictures as a rule, because I understood that I had a responsibility to the people who were my viewers – without them, I wouldn't have my career – so I always tried to be friendly and approachable, and I often indulged in a bit of chitchat. People were generally lovely to me – friendly and complimentary about the show and how much they loved it.

The viewers had quickly picked up on my language. I'd always talked on the show as I would in real life. I called breasts 'bangers' and told my ladies we were going to use 'knicker know-how'. This became the public's way of communicating with me. I was standing on Oxford Street one day when a taxi drove past me with two women hanging out of the window, both with their tops pulled up showing their bras, screaming, 'Grab my BANGERS, Auntie Gok!' I laughed for about a week!

But fame had started to change the dynamics of my friendships. It was now impossible to go on a night out with mates and not be approached all evening for autographs and pictures. Rightly, my friends were frustrated with the constant attention I was getting. They weren't jealous of the fame, they simply didn't want to share the time we had together with the rest of the country.

While I tried to be polite and do what I could for people who wanted autographs and photos, sometimes it just wasn't possible because I had a life to live as well. One night, E'lain and I had gone out for a drink and ended up having an argument as we stood on Shaftesbury Avenue. It was pretty intense and we were trying to work things out, both of us in tears, when a couple stopped and asked if they could have their picture taken with me. They could see we were both upset, but it didn't stop them. For the first time I said no, saying I was sorry but it was a really bad time. The man called me a wanker and as they walked off, the woman said, 'I knew he wasn't like he is on TV, what a fucking fake!'

I couldn't believe it and was left even more upset than I had been in the first place. I realised that fame had now eaten its way into my personal life. After this episode, I promised myself I would do as much as humanly possible to protect my family and friends from this new world of mine.

There were other changes, too. For the first time in my life, I began to have some proper money. When I'd first started on *How To Look Good Naked* I was earning less than I had been as a stylist, but this was now improving. My sponsorships, my books (I'd signed up to do two more style books) and the success of the show were starting to bring in some good money, and I was looking at other business possibilities, such as my own underwear line. It was a strange feeling after being skint for most of my life, but my approach to it all was not to go out and splurge.

My working-class caution was too ingrained for that and I continued living frugally. I bought a few nice things, and allowed myself a good car and some designer clothes – but my rule was that everything had to be paid for upfront. No credit. I knew that TV presenters could have a short shelf life, and I was too frightened that it all might come to an end and leave me with nothing to start wasting my hard-earned money. I carried on renting flats and saved up my cash because I wasn't going to buy a property until I could afford it outright.

With series two, viewing figures had grown and Channel 4 knew they had a winner on their hands. We were soon back in production for series three, now with even more episodes per series. Maverick had also worked hard on developing my relationship with them. Alex Fraser, Maverick's creative director, became my confidante when I was unsure about an editorial decision. She always convinced me the producers were right, but just the fact she listened to me made me feel she had my interests at heart.

The press continued to support us, and *Naked* was still being picked up by other countries. Australia, New Zealand, Canada and Poland – to name but a few – had bought the show, and our message of 'Size hero, not size zero' was being preached round the globe and in many different languages. It was a strange feeling to think that people in countries I had never visited knew who I was!

I developed various strategies so that I could lead as normal a life as possible. I began to customise my routines. Shopping trips into central London were strictly limited to the 9 till 10 a.m. slot when the stores would be virtually deserted. When I needed clothes, I would run into Topshop and grab a whole load of stuff and buy it quickly so that no one had time to recognise me. I also styled up a disguise of tracksuit, cap and sunglasses to assist in making my visits to Sainsbury's less interrupted. No one needs an audience when deciding which toilet roll to buy.

But as *How To Look Good Naked* became a prime-time phenomenon, I had to come to terms with the fact that I'd entered the next phase of celebrity. It wasn't simply a matter of being hassled – it was now more serious than that.

One example of this was when a friend of mine had managed to get a couple of tickets for the *Spice Girls'* comeback tour at the O2. He asked me if I wanted to go with him and, of course, I agreed. I didn't consider where we might be sitting; I was too excited to be seeing the girls' costumes.

When we arrived at the O2, I realised I might have made a mistake. Getting into the building was like trying to get through a football match riot. Mothers and daughters rushed me for autographs and pictures, and the more people that crowded us, the more attention I received.

Once we were finally in the building, drinks bought and popcorn stashed, we went to find our seats. The tickets were amazing! We had a fabulous view of the stage, right in the centre of the main circle. As we walked towards our seats, the most enormous cheering erupted round us. I thought the girls had arrived on stage early, although that was strange since the house lights had not gone down. I very quickly realised that it wasn't the Spice Girls the entire arena was cheering for, it was ME!

Within moments, a swarm of people had rushed towards us again; it was incredible! Camera flashes popped in every direction, a chanting of 'Gok, Gok, Gok ...' filled my ears and hundreds of Spice Girl programmes were being thrust towards me for my signature. Luckily, the security guards had clocked this situation and pulled me and my friend from the crowds. We were placed in a private box to stop any danger to Health and Safety in the arena. We were gutted, however, as the private box had the worst view of the stage! If I didn't know it before, I certainly knew it now – *Naked* mania had arrived.

Zigazig ah!

A few more episodes like this made me realise that my safety – and my friends' – could be at risk if I didn't take more precautions. I was mobbed at airports, and going into clubs and restaurants became a nightmare. One night in Liverpool, I went out to a club with some of the team and we ended up having to leap over the bar and run out the back to prevent ourselves from being squashed. After that, I knew I would have to be more sensible.

Nights out with mates were now organised like military events, with VIP areas booked and doormen warned of our arrival. Hotels were given a pseudonym to stop the staff from telling their friends about my stay (this was after a receptionist told her best mate, who then told the whole town that I was staying in the hotel. After checking in, I went to my room and was greeted by four girls, who had camped outside my door waiting for photographs and signatures!).

Filming the show also had to be carefully organised. No longer could we slip discreetly into a store and not be noticed beyond the odd curious glance. Security guards were now booked to help usher the hundreds of fans who wanted to watch us film – and it's hard to concentrate with camera flashes and kids screaming your name.

There were other aspects of fame I hadn't expected – the downsides that went beyond simply losing my privacy. Meeting guys was no longer a simple 'Fancy a drink?' or 'Do you come here often?' Potential dates needed to be vetted with expert precision to ensure honesty and the right intentions. I had spent my life not really attracting too much male attention, and all of a sudden I was inundated with offers from men who wanted to 'get to know me better' – only to discover their tender would be laced with lies about their profession, maritial status and age. On the other hand, I was also committed to making sure that past, current or potential boyfriends would not be subjected to public scrutiny, even if it had become a part of my daily schedule.

Friends would email me and ask if I knew that there were t-shirts for sale with my picture on them, or that I was featured on birthday cards and unofficial calendars. I would hear myself talked about on the radio or my name would crop up in conversation between characters in *Coronation Street*, *Hollyoaks* and *EastEnders*, or in comedy shows. I had entered the national consciousness to the point where my name became synonymous with a kind of caring campness. I discovered that someone was working as me at a lookalike agency, going along to birthday parties and hen nights and whatever, being paid to pretend to be me. I have to say, that freaked me out.

My family was inevitably caught up in the ripple effects of my fame. While I'd been following my path through make-up to styling and then on to television, my family had been pursuing their own lives.

After university, Oilen had fulfilled her academic promise and had become a solicitor specialising in child-care cases, a world far removed from mine. Of course,

Oilen has to keep the details of her work confidential, but I know how much good she is doing saving families and young children from danger, and I feel humbled and honoured to call her my sister.

It took Kwok-Lyn a little while longer to discover what he wanted, but when he did, it was amazing. He had managed to keep his head above water, getting through college and then working in the restaurant, and not falling into crime or loafing round town like so many other kids with similar backgrounds to us. Instead, in a weird mirroring of my father's life, he left Leicester for a year, going to Portsmouth to work, and returning with his gorgeous wife, Lisa. When he got back, he was reinvented and ready to take on the role of eldest son.

It wasn't easy for Lisa to find her place in our fold. It took her years of patience and determination to break the watertight seal surrounding our family, but I'm happy that she did. Lisa has shown us that we can, as a family, exist around other people. She has undoubtedly added a new layer to our lives.

As Kwok-Lyn and Lisa began to raise their two gorgeous daughters, Maya-Lily and Lola-Rose, Kwok-Lyn found the path he'd been searching for and became a martial arts instructor and specialist. He created his own business and discovered he had a masterful business brain. He wrote for combat magazines, taught in America and started up one of the country's biggest martial arts expos at the NEC, which he runs every year.

He is incredibly well respected in his field, but by none more than me.

Mum and Dad had finally closed The Gong and had moved out of Chinese food altogether. Instead they took on a fish and chip shop called the Whetstone Fish Bar and they carried on working as hard as they ever did, running their business six days a week.

When I started to appear on the television, they were very excited for me and watched every minute of it … twice! Mum and Dad decorated the chip shop with pictures of me, and cuttings from magazines and papers about the show. I was now able to afford to treat them to some holidays, which I loved doing.

But my fame had its downside for the family, too. Oilen found that she was suddenly known as 'the sister of' instead of as a person in her own right, which was rightly frustrating for her. My parents were constantly asked about me by customers, and their friends and friends of friends were forever requesting books, autographs and merchandise. They hated letting anyone down, so when I went home, I would find a great pile of books and pictures by my bed ready for signing.

Nor could I enjoy time alone with my family any more. On the rare occasion when I made it home to Leicester, most of our socialising and catching up was done in my uncle's restaurant eating dim sum, just as we always had done. But long-gone were the days when we could overorder, scoff our faces and be left alone together. We were now mobbed by 'old friends' of the family or distant relatives, who wanted autographs or a quick picture.

My family was very gracious and would always stand aside for me to have my picture taken but secretly I resented it. I didn't mind having photos taken, doing autographs or chatting at any time other than when I was with my family. My life had become so busy that the small amount of time I had with them had become as precious as diamonds to me. I felt obliged to sign the bits of serviettes or pose for the photos and very seldom would I say no, but I felt guilty when I did.

I wanted to go home precisely so that I could get away from the madness of fame and my TV life. I didn't want to be working there, too, so I made a rule that I wouldn't do any signing at home. But my mum would always come sneaking in last thing with a book and a pen, begging for just one signature so she didn't have to disappoint someone, which I understood but couldn't help finding frustrating. Like I said, fame is a head-fuck.

It was my business-brained brother who coped best. He realised that he couldn't stop all this from happening, so reckoned he might as well turn it to his advantage. He's worked me hard, pimping me out to help his business and using my fame as much as he can. Brilliant! Go, Kwok-Lyn. I don't mind – in a small way, it feels like repayment for the meals he and Lisa fed me when I was ill. Fame is an ongoing situation that we've learned to cope with as best we can. I'm still a son and brother before I'm anything else, and if it all goes away tomorrow, my precious family will still be there, loving me just the same, no matter what. I know what they put up with for my sake, and I love them all the more for coping with it.

Comfort Risotto

INGREDIENTS

1 pack of bacon
1 onion
1 oz butter
10 oz risotto rice
1 pack of cherry tomatoes
1 ¼ pint chicken or vegetable stock
2 oz Parmesan

METHOD

Heat oven to 200°C/gas mark 6. Chop bacon into small pieces and fry in a casserole dish until crispy, then add the onion and butter. Cook for 3 minutes, then add the risotto rice and stir. Add the cherry tomatoes and the hot stock, cover with the lid and bake for around 20 minutes. Stir it through again and grate the Parmesan on top.

Total comfort on a plate!

Recipe by: Make-up artist extraordinaire, Charlie 'Pleasure' Duffy

CHAPTER TWENTY-SIX

A New Dawn

I had almost given up my styling work to devote my time to making the show, but when Carol told me that French and Saunders wanted me to style them for their 25th birthday anniversary at the BBC, I jumped at the chance.

I'd always been a huge F&S fan. Simply having the opportunity to meet the girls would have been enough, but to get to style them was like a dream come true. I had followed their career since it began back in the eighties with their sitcom *Girls On Top* and my time at Central had been made more bearable by the thought that they had attended the school and even been on my course – fuck, I was a super fan! Who would have thought that one day these great comedy icons would ask me to style them?

The girls booked me for all the shoots they had in the lead-up to the anniversary. Every magazine and weekend supplement wanted to interview them and, of course, they needed pictures.

Dawn's manager told Carol it would probably be a good idea if I went to Dawn's house and had a rummage through her wardrobe, as she had her own clothing line and had a fabulous collection of outfits.

Oh my God! Someone pinch me! How exciting!

I geared myself up and set off to Reading, where Dawn lived with Lenny Henry. Their house was hidden in beautiful, picture-postcard-perfect countryside. As I drove up the gravelled driveway towards their house – described to me as a 'cottage' – nerves began to make me giddy. The house was far grander than a regular cottage but it still retained a natural, rural feel – not unlike a house from *The Vicar of Dibley*. Wisteria climbed up its walls, perfectly complementing the manicured garden.

As I made my way to the front door, I stopped for a moment to gather my confidence and have a quick rehearsal of my greeting: 'Hi Dawn, I'm Gok', or 'Hello, Ms French, I'm Gok ...'

Before I had time to knock, the door opened just far enough for Dawn to pop her head out: 'Hello, Gok Wan!' she said, with the biggest, warmest smile I have ever seen. She swung the door open and before I had a chance to say 'Hi' back to her, Dawn leaped from her doorstep, wrapped her arms round me and gave me the biggest hug and kiss in the world.

OMG ... the Vicar of Dibley just kissed me. *Praise the Lord!*

I tried to keep my cool but it was hard not to be starstruck. With a beaming smile and slightly flushed cheeks, I walked into her home. It was as if Dawn had known me for years as she led the way to her kitchen, offered me a cup of tea and asked if I was hungry. Her easy-going charm and warm hospitality totally put me at my ease and I only just managed to stop myself from blurting out how much I admired her. After a mug of very sugary tea and a couple of chocolate bourbons, we decided it was time to take a look at her wardrobe.

Before I'd put down my mug, Dawn rushed out of the kitchen screaming, 'Come on, Gok Wan!' (I loved the way Dawn used my full name; it made me giggle.) I followed her into the hallway and suddenly there she was at the top of the staircase, her top off and the cheekiest of smiles on her face!

I burst into fits of laughter. Was this really happening? It was as if this scene was a sketch from one of her shows and I was Dawn's stooge! Then, with such perfect timing it was almost as though it'd been choreographed, the front door opened and in walked Lenny bloody Henry! Rooted to the spot, I grinned inanely at him, gestured to his wife by way of explaining my presence in his hallway, and said, 'Hi, Lenny, I'm Gok.'

I was blushing like a child who'd been caught by his parents kissing the babysitter. With an equally cheeky smile, Lenny replied, 'Hi, Gok, what are you doing with my wife?' Then he walked into the kitchen, laughing to himself.

I LOVED THIS HOUSE!

Our afternoon was like a dream slumber party. Dawn tried on a million outfits while I lounged on her bed critiquing her clothes. We got on famously. Dawn made me feel totally comfortable in her home and spoke to me as if I was a member of her family. I was so in awe of her that when she told me she loved *Naked* and admired what the show had done for women all round the country, I burned with pride!

After we'd gone through Dawn's huge walk-in wardrobe, she said she had something special to show me. She led me to the spare room, where she had a closet filled with old costumes from her amazing comedic career. It was like flicking through fashion porn! I almost cried when she pulled out her vicar's robe and crucifix.

My time with Dawn and Jennifer was amazing. I didn't get to meet Jennifer until the first shoot we did but, just as Dawn had been, Jennifer was simply gorgeous and welcoming in her own way. Where Dawn was ballsy and upfront, Jennifer was softer and more reserved. When I suggested what Jennifer should wear from the rails of clothes I had prepped, she thought about the clothes more methodically than Dawn did and seemed to have a more cautious approach to her wardrobe. Perhaps her research for *Absolutely Fabulous* had given her a greater understanding of how clothes can instantly work for or against you. This was made apparent by how she decided if she liked or disliked one of my suggestions. She knew what clothes suited her body shape and she also knew what she wanted to wear.

Jen was definitely the calmer of the two and allowed Dawn to deliver most of the punch lines, both on and off set. I loved how they had allowed their relationship to evolve over the last twenty-five years and how it still worked like a faithful tandem bicycle.

When we'd finished our press run, the girls invited me to their last live show at the Drury Lane Theatre. They performed amazingly and were fabulously hospitable to me at the after-show party, introducing me to their families and close friends. Meeting and working with the girls was definitely a huge career highlight for me. For a brief moment, I imagined myself to be a girl who had hit the top.

Dawn gave me one piece of advice I will always remember: 'You always have control. It may not feel like it, but you do.'

As we filmed series three of *Naked*, I had never felt more confident of my work. We were still re-working the format every series, as it was important to keep refreshing it so that it didn't become tired and formulaic. Besides, our ladies always thought they knew what to expect because they'd seen previous series, and we wanted to make sure they were taken by surprise. In series three, we went a step further and asked our ladies to go on the catwalk not just in their underwear with their naked picture displayed above, but actually naked. It was a lot to ask, and I was worried we might have gone too far, but as usual my girls did me proud.

How To Look Good Naked is actually built in a huge way on humour. I would gently tease my girls because even though I was building up confidence, I couldn't be too smarmy or so compassionate it spilled over into cloying sentiment. Humour helped me to lead the ladies to question themselves, and to see the funny side of the situation. It also helped to lighten the really quite terrifying prospect of getting naked on national television.

I had always been in awe of television comedians who could deliver great gags with perfect timing and when I was younger, I would try to learn from them. At school, ever on the quest to make people laugh, I would listen carefully to conversations and look for places I could jump in and shock, or finish the story with an unexpected, amusing ending. It all proved to be perfect training for my job.

I loved using my sense of humour while I was presenting – the gags and stunts that were very funny. It felt like I was contributing more to the show than just my knowledge of fashion. The more I made my ladies laugh, the better our performance was on screen.

I also developed my live comedic skills when we filmed the catwalk shows. In one day, we would film four catwalks and we could have in excess of 8,000 audience members who would tirelessly stand all day and watch the shows. We needed the audience to be upbeat and join in, clapping and cheering, so we warmed them up before we started to film. I would go out on to the stage for about fifteen minutes and talk to the audience. I loved it! I'd crack gags, flirt, do some gentle teasing and get them all laughing and cheering. It was the best buzz in the world. I absolutely loved being in front a live audience and I loved experimenting with my improvisation skills. It was the actor inside me who was finally getting a chance to come out and play.

These skills also came in handy for the live work I was doing outside *Naked*. Whether Jonathan Ross was interviewing me in front of a live studio audience, or I was hosting an awards ceremony, as people had started to ask me to do, live audience work was where I was happiest.

Towards the end of 2007, Maverick called Carol and me into their offices to pitch an idea to us. They wanted me to consider doing a live stage show of *How To Look Good Naked*.

Live shows had proven to be a great way of supporting a TV brand. *Top Gear*'s live show had been a great success and *Strictly Come Dancing* and *The X Factor* were exploring the concept as well. I was nervous because it was something I had never done before but I knew that I couldn't pass up this opportunity to test these skills and see whether I was up to the challenge. So I said yes, what the hell, I'd do it.

We decided we would take some of the elements of *Naked* and develop them into a live performance: cutting up clothes to demonstrate how to show off your silhouette; hair and make-up transformations; a five-part catwalk show and, of course, a naked finale. We'd also have a live question-and-answers session with the audience and as much humour as I could muster as I shook in my size-nine boots! I was absolutely petrified. What if the tickets didn't sell? What if people walked out because they were bored? What if I wasn't funny enough to host a two-hour live show?

The production company decided we should hold the show in Glasgow as the company was based there, and they knew the audience would be lively. Happily, the tickets sold out, and before I knew it there was no turning back.

The lead-up to the show was intense. My nerves kept me from sleeping and when I did sleep, I had nightmares that I was booed off the stage. I couldn't help feeling I had bitten off more than I could chew, but my fear of failure meant I wasn't prepared to back out.

On the day of the live show, the technical crew had a complete run-through of the lighting and sound cues, and their rehearsal overran by more than two hours due to a lighting disaster. As time ticked on, I grew more and more frantic. I didn't care if I couldn't be lit on stage, I just wanted – no, *needed* – a couple of rehearsals. But there was no time. By 4 p.m., I still hadn't had a full run-through of the show and my nerves were frayed beyond repair. Carol and my parents were there, but there was no way anyone could calm me down I was feeling so frantic.

At 5 p.m. I was able to block the show through – basically run through all my exits and entrances and where I needed to be and when – but there was not enough time for a full rehearsal.

I sat in my dressing room, shallow breathing and feeling desperate. Then I reminded myself that this was the kind of thing professional actors had to deal with. And what did they do? No matter how nervous and terrified they were, they went out there and did it. They winged it, relying on their innate talent and the knowledge that things could go quite wrong and often the audience would be none the wiser. I would have to call on all my experience and all my resources. Fuck! Could I do it?

By 7 p.m., the stage manager was giving me my half-hour call. I decided that this was the worst day of my life. I couldn't remember the sequence of the show, I couldn't remember my lines and the earpiece they had given me so that I could hear the director was falling out of my sweaty nervous ear.

I was about to go on stage in front of thousands of PAYING people and die!

Standing backstage and looking out of the wings was the most horrendous experience of my life. The theatre was packed to capacity with people, including groups of tipsy women who were all chanting my name. I wanted to vomit.

Suddenly, the introduction music began to play and smoke filled the stage. The 'voice of God' began to introduce me and I took my position at the centre of the stage, hidden by two huge, floor-to-ceiling, red velvet curtains.

'Ladies and Ladies ... Please be upstanding for your host for the evening ... He's the Sultan of Style, the Master of all Makeovers and your best mate ... Get your bangers ready ... It's GOK WAN ...!'

The audience went absolutely berserk. They screamed, shouted, clapped and chanted my name so loudly, it reverberated through my chest. The curtains lifted, more smoke poured from behind me and a giant spotlight hit me. My silhouette filled the entire stage as well as the two enormous screens to the sides of the stage. I stood in the centre of the stage with my back to the audience while they shouted and chanted my name ever louder. My heart was beating like a drum, and my arms and legs shook with excitement. This was what I had dreamed of all my life – to be on stage in front of a live audience.

As I slowly turned round and faced the audience, I remember thinking, *If you die right now, then it serves you fucking right, you silly twat!*

The show was ... INCREDIBLE! The first half ran twenty minutes too short as my nerves made me race through the schedule, but I made the time up in the question-and-answer session. The audience remained engaged throughout the entire show, laughing and crying in all the right places. The makeovers were a triumph and the catwalk finale got the entire audience out of their seats, dancing and singing. When I did a saucy semi-strip, taking my pants off from under a black leather kilt, they went absolutely mad. The audience was amazing, every single one of them!

WHAT A FUCKING BUZZ!

Another highlight was when I was asked to present live from the *Sex And The City* premiere at Leicester Square. I couldn't believe it!

I'm a self-confessed *SATC* addict. I have watched every single episode at least a hundred times and, like so many women in the world, I live my life by the girls' mantra: Fuck it and let's go shopping.

I adore everything about the show: the costumes, the situations and, of course, the 'girlfriend' camaraderie. I was so excited to be chosen to present one of the most anticipated premieres ever! *Thank you, Father, Son and Holy Chanel!*

On the day of the premiere, I'd been filming all day on *Naked*. When I arrived at Leicester Square at 5 p.m., dressed head to toe in Vivienne Westwood, I was exhausted.

No sooner had I put my manbag down, I was being given cue cards, scripts, directions and a double cappuccino. By 6 p.m., the square was filled to capacity with hysterical *SATC* fans (myself included).

I discovered that I was the only presenter allowed on the red carpet so it was my responsibility to interview *all* the main cast (OMG – SJP!), the director, producers and all the A-listers. It was like I had won the lottery.

As I rehearsed my opening link, it suddenly dawned on me that I had never presented a red-carpet event before, and what the hell was I supposed to do? What if I ran out of questions to ask the girls? What if they hated me? What if I went to double kiss one of the girls and they only wanted one? What if I forgot Sarah's real name and called her Carrie? My mind was filled to bursting point with 'What if's', but there was simply no time to get too nervous.

At any red-carpet event, the cast is expected to spend as much time with the fans as possible and as little time as they can with the journalists, without appearing rude. My director told me I needed to keep the girls talking for as long as humanly possible since they were our 'money shots'. If the PRs tried to pull the girls away early, I had to continue interviewing them until the very last second. There was only one chance to make a connection in the interview and since we were making the only official premiere show for the UK market, it was imperative the interviews were interesting and informative. No pressure then!

Flustered and panicked, I was shooting the first few links but I was finding it hard to concentrate, which made my presenting look like the video recording for my GCSE Media Studies. Just then, through the masses of PRs, security guards, hysterical fans and nervous film execs, I saw it. Like a gorgeous green bird of paradise, Sarah Jessica's Philip Treacy hat rose from a blacked-out Mercedes.

I thought I was going to be sick with nerves and excitement. Sarah Jessica 'the Goddess' Parker was now standing on the same red carpet as me, waving to thousands of screaming fans. She looked amazing in a knee-length silk tulle, flared chiffon dress by Alexander McQueen, and her hat was a magnificent confection of a green silk rose, meadow flowers and butterflies.

The square had erupted. I have never heard cheering like it. It was like being at the fashion World Cup! I found myself grinning madly and clapping like a idiotic seal when I saw her, until my director quizzically shook his head at me, urging me to try and control myself – *shame!*

*

As she worked the crowds of photographers and fans, I waited obediently at my camera for my chance to interview her. The longer I waited, the more nervous I became, my hands shaking with total euphoria.

After half an hour, Sarah Jessica finally arrived next to me. She was tiny but perfect in every single way. I couldn't believe I was standing next to Carrie Bradshaw! I wanted to scream, 'I LOVE YOU!' down her neat little ear and then hold her until the last day of eternity, but I guessed the security guards would probably pull me to the ground and Taser me to death before that happened.

The questions on my cue cards that I'd been rehearsing for hours seemed to melt away and all I could do was look at her. I wanted to prod her on the arm and make sure she was real, but I didn't dare to touch her. This was it! My one and only chance not to balls up the best moment of my career to date. Sarah Jessica smiled at me, the camera swung round and my director screamed, 'Action!'

I was smiling so hard I must have looked like deranged, but I managed to hold it together just long enough to get my first question out: 'Sarah Jessica, you look amazing, darling! Who are you wearing?"

The interview lasted about three minutes. What I asked after my first question is beyond me; I was trapped in a star-struck womb where I could only hear the sound of my own beating heart. Before she was whisked away to the photographers, she turned to me, placed her hand on my arm and said, 'Thanks, Gok, that was a nice interview. I hope you like the film.'

Fuck me backwards with a plastic fish slice! I LOVE YOU, SJP!

Over the next hour I interviewed Kristin, Cynthia, Kim, Michael and a handful of very groomed celebrities. Patricia Field, the *SATC* stylist, recognised me as her British equivalent; Vivienne noticed I was dressed head to toe in her gear; and Davina McCall hugged me so hard, I think I may have farted. It was truly a fabulous evening.

After that night, I realised I'd found a confidence with my work I never thought I would achieve. Perhaps I was never going to be the best presenter in the world, but now I'd been in some demanding situations and I'd managed to rise to the occasion. At last I began to trust that I could do this job. Maybe now I could relax a little bit and let myself be happy.

'Last night I got to thinking, when does meeting SJP ever stop being an OMG ... ?'

CHAPTER TWENTY-SEVEN

Wooooaaah – Fashion!

When Carol called and told me Channel 4 wanted a meeting with me, I assumed it was to speak about *Naked*. I thought they might want to thrash around the format and see if there were any ideas I could contribute to re-developing it.

So I was completely blown away when they told me they wanted me to host a different show called *Gok's Fashion Fix*. My initial reaction was WOW! I was excited and pleased in equal measure that the channel thought me experienced enough to carry two of their shows. This could be just what my career needed as I'd become very comfortable with *Naked*. I was far from bored but I was aware that a new challenge would be good for me. The channel offered a few days for me to think about it before they would give the production company sign-off confirmation.

After my excitement wore off, I began to consider the downsides. What if *Fashion Fix* wasn't as good as *Naked*? What if the viewers hated me for trying my hand at another show? What if *Fashion Fix* flopped like an eighties fringe?

I wondered if this show was too much, too soon. After all, I'd only just found my feet with my presenting career and *Naked* was still getting top ratings for the channel. Did I need a new show?

Carol and I had lunch and we discussed the pros and cons. The upside was that *Fashion Fix* would be a programme where I could show off my skills as a stylist on some real fashion situations. And I would be able to avoid being pigeonholed as only the *Naked* Gok; a new side to my personal brand might lead to a whole host of new opportunities. But there was a massive downside. They wanted me to have a co-presenter – pop princess, Alexa Chung.

What?!

I didn't think there was any way I could present with Alexa. She was a million years younger than me, a billion times prettier than me and she had a trillion times more experience shooting in a studio – I was used to out-of-studio presenting. Arghhh!!!

But I kept my fears to myself and agreed to speak to the producers and find out more about the show.

Colette Foster had moved from Maverick TV by this time, and set up her fashion TV camp at Endemol, who had come up with the idea of *Fashion Fix*. I was pleased the show had been commissioned from Colette, and as we met over a cocktail she told me what she had in mind for the series.

Fashion Fix would be a fast-paced magazine programme that celebrated all genres of fashion. The main segment would be The Fashion Face-off – four big-wigs from the world of fashion would compete against me to assemble four looks to put down the catwalk. The twist was that I would be limited to high-street fashion with a budget of £200 for each outfit, while the fashion girls would be able to spend as much as they liked on designer labels. At the end of the show, the studio audience would decide which collection they liked the best, and vote, not knowing which collection was designer and which was high street. We would also have a celebrity wardrobe inspection, a travelling catwalk where I would go to a different town in the UK searching for the country's best-dressed person, and a road test, where Alexa would put a selection of products through their paces. On top of this, there would be the designer interview, where Alexa would go to a different part of the world to interview a high-end designer – Cavalli at his villa in Florence, Lagerfeld in his iconic Rue Cambon office in Paris and so on. *How come she got to do the best job?!*

I listened carefully and then thought: ARE YOU FUCKING MAD, COLETTE?

I couldn't believe she wanted me to go head-to head-in a fashion face-off with some of the biggest names and most influential buyers in the fashion industry. They'd have a limitless budget and access to the most incredible designer labels, while I'd have my £200 and the great British high street. *Fucking suicide, girlfriend!*

I knew I was a competent stylist. I loved the British high street and I had the confidence to accept a challenge but the format did seem pretty tilted against me. How could I even think about going up against Chanel, Dolce, Halston and Choo? These designers spend thousands of pounds sourcing the best materials in the world. They have the best pattern cutters, designers and creative minds in the business. *Pass me a bucket, I feel a little queer!*

I was also concerned the audience would think I was being a hypocrite since I'd made no secret of the fact that my wardrobe was bursting with designer clobber I'd collected over the years. I love designer clothes and I didn't want the fashion industry to think I was slagging them off, telling the public they shouldn't spend their hard earned cash on high-end luxury goods.

Colette convinced me I wouldn't be rubbishing designer clothes, instead, I would be championing the high street, giving viewers who didn't have the funds to splash out on labels ideas about how to look good without breaking the bank!

I listened, thought about it from that perspective and it made sense. On *How To Look Good Naked,* we championed real women, telling them that being size 18 was no better or worse than being a size 8. *Fashion Fix* could do the same, but with clothes. The message was 'Style, whatever your budget.'

The more I thought about it, the more excited I became. I knew that I would have to get over myself long enough to build a working relationship with Alexa but, who knew, maybe I would even learn a few things. I had a feeling this show could be huge. So I cross-stitched on the dotted line.

The production on the show began and it felt strange. I was working with a new production company, a brand new team and I was presenting a new show. I couldn't have felt more out of my comfort zone.

I enjoyed the Fashion Face-offs much more than I'd expected. It was hard work and everything came from me but I got a real thrill from using my fashion nous again. The key was to give a high street item a twist, hide the details that made it look cheap, add details that made it seem more expensive and then accessorise to within an inch of its life.

I coined the phrase 'haberdashery chic' to describe what I did when I customised outfits. I'd get corsages, buttons, ribbons, braiding, trimmings, motifs – anything that would spruce up, for example, a dirt-cheap pair of gold shoes from New Look. I used belts as headbands, skirts as dresses, put tops on back to front and spray-painted handbags. I put beads on tasselled shoes, ripped sleeves off here and re-jigged hems there, puffed out with flouncy underskirts or cinched in with statement belts. Whatever the look – whether it was beachwear, summer brights, working girl, night on the town – I managed to get my looks together on the cheap and give them a designer flavour through their custom-made individuality. It was all great fun.

Originally, the customising of the outfits was going to be done off camera, but Colette loved watching how I did it and decided that it was great television. Now watching the styling magic is a signature of the show, but it nearly didn't make it on to the screen at all.

The production company had found four fashion mavens to go up against me: Marigay Mackee from Harrods (no shortage of labels there, I think you'll find), Erin Mullaney from Browns (yes, plenty of juicy designers in one of London's top boutiques), Lina Basma from Selfridges (the spiritual home of fashionistas) and Brix Smith-Start from the Start boutique. All these ladies had to do was waft about, selecting the latest and most gorgeous designer dresses, with their acres of luxurious fabric, the finest shoes and the most outrageously expensive bags and jewellery, and *voilà*. While I was still sweating over a hot needle and a spray-starch can, they would be taking the weight of their Louboutins with a well-deserved martini.

When I wasn't doing that, I was racing about with celebrities. In the first series I met Geri Halliwell, Kelly Osbourne (who confessed she'd once spent $28,000 dollars on a coat – and she'd never worn it), Mischa Barton, Dannii Minogue, Lorraine Kelly (my gorgeous TV mum whose episode pulled in huge ratings as we rolled around on her bed), Lulu and Jamelia.

But the most exciting moment for me was meeting Joan Collins.

Joan was priceless. She agreed to do the show but we had to travel to San Tropez to film her. It was arranged that I'd meet her in the small town and, as her wardrobes were far away in London and New York, we'd go shopping together, so we could see her passion for couture and high-end brands in action.

The producers had arranged for us to meet at the big clock in the centre of town and from there we would hit the very expensive shops. On the day, in true Hollywood style, Joan was running late, which did not help my already frayed nerves. The heat was unbearable and I was dressed in my uniform of black jacket and skinnies – not the kind of clothes I recommend you wear while cavorting in the midday heat and cobbled streets of the south of France with TV legend Alexis Colby!

After what felt like years, a battered old people carrier rolled up (it was not dissimilar to an unlicensed minicab in Soho on a Friday night). The windows were tinted but I could just make out the most enormous white straw hat on top of a very heavily made-up Ms Joan Collins, who was sitting in the back seat. I opened the door with a very shaky hand, waited for Joan to alight, then greeted her with the obligatory double kiss, careful not to touch flesh. She lowered her head, lifted her sunglasses and said, 'Hello, darling, I knew you'd be wearing more make-up than me!'

With that she flicked her hair and strutted off, Percy (her husband/manager) in tow.

The afternoon was fabulous. We browsed casually in the local boutiques and chatted about her career in Hollywood, love life and, of course, her passion for style. She soon opened up to me and her stories were fascinating. It was as if she had always existed in the spotlight: she oozed glamour, sophistication and confidence.

As we roamed the streets of Saint Tropez, I was surprised by the lack of attention she attracted. This is Joan fucking Collins! I wanted to shout. How can you not want an autograph or picture? But it was as if she was a local, just out shopping for some bog roll before she went home to prepare lunch for good old Percy, who kept three metres away at all times and only spoke when he was instructed to. I desperately wanted people to fall apart in shock at the sight of Joan shopping but no one really did. The occasional 'Salut, Joan!' was shouted and a couple of Brits asked for a picture but that was pretty much it. How disappointing! I think my ego was more bruised than hers, as I so wanted to show off the fact I was Joan's new bitch, but I never got the opportunity.

About three hours into filming, I began to find my confidence: Joan was no longer the untouchable screen goddess I had built her up to be; she had become a telly friend. She chatted with me like we'd known each other the whole of our lives and at one point she actually looked me in the eyes. We shared a couple of jokes on camera and found a comfortable and steady rhythm. I was getting somewhere! Finally, we reached our final shop, Roberto Cavalli.

The crew was exhausted, I was exhausted, but Joan was still firing on all cylinders. The director, Ann Wilson, instructed me to wrap the interview up, so it was my last opportunity to ask Joan any final questions about her life as a style icon. We sat down in the store on a very camp purple pouffe and began the 'out-tro'.

'So, Joan, have you enjoyed today?'

'Yes, darling, it's been fabulous!'

'Have you learned anything from your Auntie Gok?'

'Darling, you have taught me nothing. Have I taught you anything?'

'Yes, Joan, you have taught me how to be a diva for the day, thank you so much!'

'You're welcome, Gok!'

We embraced as Ann shouted, 'Cut!'

Joan then turned to me and said, 'When will this be on the BBC?'

'Joan, this is for Channel 4. Do you even know who I am?'

The whole thing was an absolute scream and I came away more a Joanie admirer than ever.

I began to realise that I was seriously exhausted. My feet had not touched the ground since I had begun filming the first series of *Naked* – I was now on my fourth show. I'd followed up my first book with another called *How to Dress*. I'd also designed a collection of underwear, endorsed glasses for SpecSavers and been to Australia on a promotional tour. I'd hosted awards shows, bought my first flat, been on every chat show in the UK, tried to maintain a social life and I was writing two fashion columns.

I was well and truly shattered. I wanted to tell Carol I was feeling the strain but I didn't because I was afraid she might think I needed to slow down. I couldn't do that – my job needed me. And the more work I was offered, the bigger the buzz I was getting. My addiction to overeating, undereating and always trying to please had now metamorphosed into a work addiction. As long as I was being called out to work at 7 a.m. and not getting home until midnight, I was being needed. I pushed myself physically and mentally and if at times it felt as though I was suffocating with pressure, at least I was in control. I ignored my body's cries of exhaustion and decided I would work as hard as I could to get the series finished and then speak to Carol about booking some time out.

Before long, we were nearing the end of production. I had managed to fight my insecurities and build a good on-screen bond with Alexa and I have to say, she taught me a lot about presenting in a studio.

The Fashion Face-offs were a huge success – soon to become everyone's favourite part of the show and the *Fashion Fix* signature – and I won every one! It was great to be able to show the viewers how to become their own stylists and not have to spend a fortune to look a million dollars. The very first face-off had the designers spending £13,000 against my £750. I still won ... credit crunch couture, baby!

The production ran over by a couple of weeks and we were still filming when the first episode aired. I was nervous about what the critics might say.

The morning after the first broadcast, I walked into the studio, dumped my bags in my dressing room and headed straight for the newspapers.

Once again, I was gutted. We'd had a mixture of reviews and most of the critics who supported *Naked* loved the show, but a couple of the broadsheets were not in agreement. It didn't matter how many good reviews we got; as always, it was the bad ones that stuck in my side like a rusty old nail. One critic wrote something along the lines of, 'Has Gok had his moment?'

WHAT? I had only been on TV for two years and already they were wondering if my star was beginning to fade! Luckily the viewing figures had been very healthy and didn't reflect the doubts of some of the higher-brow critics.

I didn't want the bad reviews to bother me but I couldn't help it. It was so difficult to read negative stuff when we'd worked so hard to produce an entertaining and informative show with a bit of jeopardy, a bit of information and heaps of glamour, but we still couldn't please them. I was so tired and for a brief moment it didn't feel worth it.

My worrying began to knock me down but after several conversations with Carol and my family, I decided I had done as much as I could. I would just have to accept the fact that some people were going to love both shows, some just one and some none.

CHAPTER TWENTY-EIGHT

Dressing Mum

The only time I have ever dressed a member of my family is when I invited Mum and Dad to an awards ceremony I was hosting. I'd spoken to Mum a few times about it and she had told me she was nervous about what to wear. I told her to buy something and I would send her the money as a treat.

As the awards got closer, I asked her if she had found something and she said no. Then it clicked: Mum wanted me to dress her but she was too proud to ask.

The weekend before the awards I cancelled my weekend plans and returned home to Leicester. I packed Mum and Dad up in the back of the car and off we drove to Marks & Spencer on a quest to dress Momma Wan.

The store was packed. I don't know how it had happened but everyone seemed to know we were coming.

We entered the shop to what felt like applause. Hurrying Mum and Dad through the crowds, I figured we would be safer if we kept moving and spent as much time in the safety of the changing rooms as possible. I grabbed an armful of dresses and dragged Momma Wan into the fitting area, leaving Dad to stroll round the suits (Dad had decided it wasn't fair Mum was getting an outfit and he wasn't. Oh, how the roles had changed!).

Once in the fitting room, it was clear Mum needed the help of some support underwear.

'Stay here while I go and get some big pants,' I told her, 'and cover yourself up, for crying out loud!'

I left her giggling in the changing room. On the shop floor, I made a beeline for the underwear section. Just as I got to the fascinators and handbags, a woman jumped out at me armed with a mobile phone and a pen and paper. Before she could ask me for a picture, I said, 'I am so sorry but I have left my mum in the changing room with just her bra and knickers on and I need to get back to her with some big pants ...' As I smiled and went to walk past her, she grabbed my arm with a wrestler's grip and snarled at me, 'I don't care, I want a picture, you rude bastard!'

I could not believe it! How could anyone speak to a total stranger like that?

I stopped, spun on my Cuban heel and glared at her, saying, 'I told you, I am with my mother and she is far more important than your bloody picture, now let go of my arm!'

The woman was shocked by my response and it obviously pissed her off because she let go of her grip and said, 'You're nothing like what you are on TV! Well, you've just lost a viewer here, love!'

Now, I know I have a public job and I know that without the viewers I do not have a career. But come on – when my mum is standing in her bra and knickers in a changing room ... Still, perhaps I was starting to feel the strain.

Dad chose the most expensive suit he could find, Mum wore the big pants and a gorgeous black cocktail dress and we all had a great night. The moral of this story is that mums need more than just big pants: they need loyal children who will always put them first.

Dear Mummy,

You are my friend. I don't know if you realise this but you are the first person I go to when I need advice. I may not always agree with you but you have the power to make my problems drift away. Your smile is the warmest place in my world and sometimes when I feel lonely, I close my eyes and imagine your smile. Over the years you've taught me how to love. I've never met anyone with so much love to give. Our family has always been an open door to anyone who needs help and that is down to you. I owe you so much for teaching me how to be kind to people around me. Do you remember when you and I picked up the Christmas tree in my Citroën 2CV, just weeks before Christmas, in the freezing cold? We rolled the roof back and squeezed the six-foot tree into the back of the car and we laughed all the way home. Whenever I'm sad, I listen out for that laugh. You will always be the centre of my world and without you it would not turn. I am proud to be your baby. You make my heart beat. I love you for a moment longer than eternity.

Babe x

As the first series of *Gok's Fashion Fix* reached the end of its broadcast, I was totally run down; most of my days were powered by nervous energy. Mum had started to get concerned about my health and our daily telephone calls were dominated with her telling me to take it easy. She advised me to tell the producers to give me a day off but, as I had done when I was sick at Central, I told her, 'I'm fine, please don't worry, really – I'm okay.'

Before I knew it, we were well into filming the new series of *How To Look Good Naked* and *Fashion Fix* had been commissioned for a second series. I couldn't tell the producers I was tired in case they thought I was either weak or a diva. Instead, I smiled as much as I could and kept my jumping around on camera to just knee height.

For the second series of *Gok's Fashion Fix,* we made some changes. Alexa was no longer my co-presenter and we brought in a whole new aspect to the show involving

GOK WAN

a member of the public who needed some help with finding out their body shape and what suited them best. *How To Look Good Naked* tackled body dysmorphia and issues of identity and confidence, with the women going on a serious emotional journey. Instead, *Fashion Fix* was unashamedly about fashion – the clothes, the shoes, the bags, the best shapes to wear and the latest trends. We came up with a new mantra for the show: 'Buy less and wear more'. I showed how, with some clever shopping and some body knowledge, it was possible to buy a capsule wardrobe of twenty-four mix and match pieces that could take any woman from work, to a meeting, to lunch with the girls, to a glamorous night out.

The celebrity aspect of the show had also subtly changed from the first series. Now I was taking label-addicted celebs and showing them how to shop from the high street. I'd dress them for a red-carpet event and dare them to wear my high-street outfit in front of the paparazzi. First up for the challenge was Janet Street Porter, who is one of the most label-loving women I've ever met – she claims it's because of her height – but all credit to her, she wore my high-street outfit to an event and duly got snapped in it. I also riffled through the wardrobes of Cilla Black, Lorraine (making her second appearance), Lynda Bellingham, Alan Carr, Ben Shephard and Ruby Wax.

The Fashion Face-off had to stay, of course. Everyone had loved it in series one, and it had become part of the

331

show's signature. But it wasn't working quite as well as we wanted. There wasn't enough at stake for it. Although I had a lot invested in the result, the ladies who had created the designer outfits in the first series didn't have quite as much riding on the outcome, as each fashionista only styled one outfit. Once they'd done their work, we didn't see them again. To introduce a bit more competition into proceedings, we decided that I would go head-to-head with only one buyer, Brix Smith-Start, although the same rules would apply – a high-street budget for me and unlimited designer spend for her.

Gok's Fashion Fix was high-octane fun that required lots of filming and lots of work with its fast pace and fun fashion elements. I loved doing it but by the end, I was even more worn out than ever.

It didn't, however, look as if I was going to get a break anytime soon, and I told myself I'd be mad to slacken off now, just when things were busier than they'd ever been.

There were some exciting challenges further down the line and I had to keep going; that was all there was to it ...

CHAPTER TWENTY-NINE

The Wake-up Call

I was busier than ever in 2009. I didn't manage to get a rest as I continued with my filming commitments; as one show finished, I went straight into production with the next. I also signed a deal with Boots to produce my own line of body products, filmed *Celebrity Apprentice* with Comic Relief, filmed a comedy sketch for Children in Need, signed a deal with Dorothy Perkins to become their online style consultant, wrote another book, *Work Your Wardrobe* and continued my commitments with SpecSavers. There was also my underwear line and other corporate jobs.

In November I signed up to make a staggering twenty-one episodes of *How To Look Good Naked* and we started work soon afterwards.

During the first few weeks of filming, I found I was suffering from painful stomach aches. Thinking that stress was giving me indigestion, I started taking a daily dose of Zantac. What I didn't realise was that my body was telling me I needed to have some time off.

One day we filmed for a couple of hours but I knew something wasn't right. My stomach was hurting and I felt more exhausted than usual. By mid-afternoon, we'd finished filming but I was too tired to leave the studio and go home, even though my driver was sitting outside waiting for me. I felt dizzy and out of breath, and it was ages before I could gather up the strength to get out to the car.

On the way home, Steve, my driver, was concerned and told me I didn't look well: I was pale and my eyes were yellow and bloodshot. As soon as I got home, I fell into bed, thinking I was just exhausted. After an hour's sleep I woke up feeling nauseous and dizzy. I ran to the toilet and vomited about two pints of sticky black sick. I knew this wasn't right but I thought that if I went to a hospital, they'd tell me it was just something I ate and I would have wasted their valuable time. Instead I got back into bed and convinced myself I could sleep it off.

Within an hour I had vomited two more times, each time producing more of this sticky black mess. I called NHS Direct and described my symptoms. The nurse immediately told me to go straight to A & E, as she suspected I was losing blood internally.

Fortunately, my flatmate Gaynor was home. We have been friends for many years; in fact, she is my oldest mate – we met back in Leicester when we were both studying at Charles Keene. I still remember seeing Gaynor's frizzy hair bouncing round the dance studio as she stag-leaped into my life. Gaynor moved to London after I promised her a shitload of nights out, a chance to make more of her life and, of course, the coveted prize of looking after me – which she has always done with great finesse.

We went to the hospital and I was so tired and ill that I fell asleep in the waiting room before my examination and was woken up by someone asking for an autograph, which was a surreal moment.

As soon as I'd been seen by a doctor, I was admitted at once. They gave me tests and blood counts, and it turned out that my haemoglobin was dangerously low. The diagnosis was exhaustion and two stomach ulcers, which had been bleeding into my stomach. I'd lost a lot of blood while I'd been ignoring my symptoms and I was taken upstairs and had an immediate blood transfusion that night. They told me that they would be pumping me full of blood for the next five days.

In the event, I ended up in hospital for two weeks, and during my stay I had six blood transfusions, two iron transfusions and was told that if I had continued to ignore the problem then it could have been fatal.

The last five years had caught up with me: I hadn't been off camera for three years and I was, quite simply, fucked. But the problem went back further than this – my stomach lining was susceptible after my years of laxative abuse, which was how I ended up with ulcers. It really was the proverbial wake-up call.

The following day I was transferred to a private room at St Thomas's with its own little bathroom, which thrilled me because I'd never stayed private before and it felt rather swanky, I must say. In fact, it felt like a bit of a holiday camp compared to my punishing work schedule. My friends sent clothes for me, and Carol came rushing over to see if I was okay and to bring me anything I needed. Even Mum and Dad came hurtling down the M1 in the Wan bus armed with bags of sweets and love.

One afternoon, after I had been hooked up to yet another bag of blood, I was lying in my room alone, feeling shattered, when I suddenly heard the most extra-ordinarily massive and endless fart coming from the next room. I think it was the longest, loudest fart possible for a human being to make. Just as I was coming to terms with that one, another came roaring out of the next room again: enormous and impressive!

I clambered out of bed with my drips attached to each arm – one of saline and one of blood – grabbed the stands and wheeled them with me into the other room to tell off whoever it was. And there, in the room next to mine, was Sir Michael *bloody* Gambon.

'Dumbledore, you dirty bastard!' I said.

Sir Michael and I spent two weeks together and we had the best time ever. He was extremely funny and great company. He'd come to my room and we'd listen to Classic FM, then we'd go out and have fags together on the roof. We weren't really allowed to but we'd chat up the nurses to persuade them to let us out, and we'd stand there together in our PJs, our drips in our arms. It was like we were having a holiday romance in hospital together.

Gradually I began to feel better and life was rather pleasant. I had lots of visits from the people I loved. My beauty products had just been launched so all the samples came in for me to play with. I got so many bunches of flowers that I amused myself by making rosettes and headbands for all the nurses, decorating their caps and uniforms with corsages.

After my two weeks of convalescing in hospital, I came home feeling a lot better. The episode made me realise that I had to calm down a bit. I told myself I would never work that hard without a break again. How could it be worth it, if it killed me? *How To Look Good Knackered?*

CHAPTER THIRTY

Changing Lives

Filming with Kelly Chamberlain was about to change my life. What made Kelly different to the other girls was that she'd had a mastectomy.

When it was first suggested it to me, my first instinct was to say, 'No'. I felt we were crossing a line into territory where we had no right to go. *How To Look Good Naked* isn't a religion, I told them, and it's not going to cure cancer. On the show we confronted basic body dysmorphia, but dealing with someone who had a disfigurement owing to a terrible disease ... well, I felt it was wrong to try and fix something as serious as that.

After much discussion, the producers convinced me to do it. I agreed, on the basis that we would take filming one day at a time and if I ever felt uncomfortable with what we were doing, I would be able to stop.

I was apprehensive. I'd never met anyone with breast cancer or who had a mastectomy, although I had done some charity work for a magazine and interviewed a woman who'd told me a bit about the difficulties of buying clothes and bras after a mastectomy operation. She'd told me about the problem of getting clothes on and off because you can't lift your arms up, about what fabrics won't hurt the skin, and we talked about how to wear a head wrap to cover up the main side effect of cancer treatment: hair loss. So I'd had a tiny bit of experience, but nothing to prepare me for this hour-long show.

Kelly had been knocked so badly by her surgery that she didn't consider herself feminine or beautiful any more, and had put all her wedding plans on hold.

As soon as I met her, I realised that although her issues were complex – I couldn't pretend she hadn't lost a breast or been badly scarred by her radiation treatment – she still responded to the same boosts as anyone else. During the course of the programme, she met other women who'd been through the same experience and come out the other side. She learned how to dress her new body and she blossomed as we progressed.

By the end, she was gorgeous, confident and ready to be a beautiful bride. For me, it was an epiphany. It reinforced how important the show could be. It was a safe place where women could go and it gave them a sense of community, whether suffering from breast cancer or body hatred. For the first time, we had been to a place where no other programme had dared to go, and it had proved inspiring. It had a powerful effect on our audience, too, and lots of good stuff came out of the show. Suddenly we were being quoted by breast cancer charities, and Kelly was asked to model for a bra company. I, also, found a lot of confidence through doing her show.

The production company went on to come up with the idea of *How To Look Good Naked – With A Difference* in which we would work with ladies who had disabilities. They'd lined up Clare, an amputee, Tracy, who was in a wheelchair, and Di, who was blind. My reaction was the same as it had been to Kelly's show. No way. I said I couldn't do it. I didn't want to pretend to be a messiah; I couldn't cure these ladies. I couldn't change them or make them well, and surely it was arrogant of me to act as though I could.

Once again, the producers talked me into it, with the same proviso. If I felt that the show wasn't working, we could stop it at any time.

I did a lot of preparation but found the whole thing very stressful and worried about it a lot. In fact, the day that we filmed the mirror moments with Clare and Tracy was the day that I fell ill and went into hospital.

After I came out, we went straight into filming the rest of the shows. It was unbelievable. It was the best decision we'd ever made and it made me fall back in love with the show all over again

Di's show, in particular, affected me a great deal. It felt like the biggest challenge of all, and I admitted that I was scared – I didn't know what it was like to be blind or live in darkness.

When we filmed the mirror moment, I felt panic. I had never before tried to help someone who couldn't see what they looked like. Di was a fifty-four-year-old who had lost her sight as a young woman so she knew what colours were like, but she had last seen patterns, fabrics and tones in the seventies. She had no idea what she looked like and she described her condition as like being locked in a box.

When Di broke down sobbing, telling me how much she hated it, I put my arms round her and held her. Although I was terribly nervous, I tried to keep calm and I managed to say, 'Instead of me being so naive as to think I could just be your eyes for you and say to you, "Well, that looks gorgeous on you", why don't we try and create our own sight between the two of us?'

Di said, 'That would be fantastic' and I knew that somehow I'd found the right approach, although I was still unsure that we'd be able to do it. I designed Di a 'style bible' based on her body shape. It allowed her to feel different clothing shapes to enable her to work out which suited her body. Its front cover had a raised silhouette of her body shape, and when she opened the book she could take out magnetised cut-outs of the jackets, shirts, dresses and skirts that most suited her shape and put them over it, so that she could 'feel' her look. Lots of textured swatches and colours (for the friends that went shopping with her) would also help remind her of what she'd learned, and the journey we'd been on together.

The whole experience helped her win back some confidence in herself and once more I really felt the power of what we were doing. It was hugely affecting to see Di re-gain something she thought she could no longer have. In a way, she began to see again – not conventionally, but mentally. She could conjure colour and shape in her mind.

Di's show was more raw than any other. There were no big whoosh sounds, no bows and bangles. Everyone went on the journey with her, and at points in the show, you could suddenly imagine what it must be like to be blind. And for Di, it meant that, just for a moment, others could feel her darkness. I think that for her that that was the most powerful thing of all.

The shows changed my world completely. They were amazing. I walked away from them thinking that *How To Look Good Naked* was now an institution and that it had proven itself not only as formatted entertainment, but as a resource show. I'm told that the Royal National Institute of the Blind now use Di's show as a training tool, and that the style book is being introduced as an aid for the blind.

To make those shows was an enormous privilege and the response we got from the disabled community was incredible. We were inundated with thank yous. I hadn't realised that there were over two million wheelchair users in this country and they have no visual representation, apart from the sign on the disabled loo. We got Shannon, a wheelchair user, into an ad campaign for Debenhams – the first time that has ever happened.

How To Look Good Naked has come so far. It has become a show that deals with extremes. It has done so much politically and achieved a huge amount: it has been spoken about in the Houses of Parliament, campaigned for plus-sized models and petitioned for body confidence to be taught in schools (Ed Balls, the then Schools Secretary, agreed to implement the policy, but we'll have to see what the future holds now there is a new government). It has evolved with the support of the public who have wanted it to do more, to change and surprise them.

Most of all, *How To Look Good Naked* has let us into other communities – the larger-sized, the disabled, the old, the frightened, the unsure, the lonely – and for a time we all feel a part of something positive. It brings us all together. It is an incredibly clever and important show, and I'm so lucky to be at the helm of it.

Had I not starved myself and suffered loneliness and body hatred, I would never have the kind of empathy I do with the people who allow us to tell their stories. *Naked* makes us feel less alone and I can't think of any other programme that does that in quite the same way. I owe so much to *Naked*, more than just giving me a job, fame and some cash. *Naked* has given me the strength to face my own body demons. I am confident my own body dysmorphia is kept at bay because of the show's empowering message.

Proper Fish and Chips

INGREDIENTS

1 telephone number of Mum and Dad's chippy
6 cans of Stella
Box of letters from your family

METHOD

Call Mum and Dad and let them know you are at the Watford Junction service station and that you'll be home in 30 minutes. Ask them to fire up the deep fat fryers. Drive the remaining 20 miles home. When you get back to Mum and Dad's house, park up, leave all your bags in the car and forget about them until later. Enter the house, kicking off your shoes. Wait for Mum to bring the fish and chips home, armed with a massive smile and a bear hug. Gorge on the salty chips and crispy fish until you feel sick. Lie back on the sofa, open a can of beer and carefully go through all the wonderful letters your family has sent you over the years. Enjoy. Rejoice. Feel full of food and love.

CHAPTER THIRTY-ONE

The View from Here

In 2008, I made a documentary called *Too Fat, Too Young* in which I met young people struggling with obesity. I also re-visited my own past – the Beaumont Leys estate, Babington Community College, even Charles Keene, where I watched a video of myself, huge and unmissable, bounding about on stage.

It was both immensely painful – more than I'd expected – and positive. It made me realise how much my past contributed to who I am today, and to my success. I suffered the worst kind of bullying as a child. It was whispered, discreet and far more personal than a public display of humiliation; it was hidden pokes and pinches that couldn't be told.

The truth is that that lost, insignificant fat boy will never leave me. I am sure the bullies had no idea that when they poked, pinched and called me names it would stay with me forever. After they had left me to cry, alone and unloved, they didn't consider what damage they had done. But today I thank them. For without the jibes and hate, I wouldn't be the person I am today.

I'm still painfully sensitive to criticism and ridicule even though I've taught myself to live it down. I still worry about gangs and walking down the street alone. I still worry about not being liked. That might seem ridiculous but sometimes, even now, I find it hard to believe that I'm successful, despite all the evidence to the contrary. When I'm watching TV or listening to the radio and they mention this Gok Wan person, it feels as if he isn't real. It feels like they're talking about a fantasy version of me, the television creation.

I'm not just that person – I hope I'm more than that. I think that person is great, and I'm very proud of him and what he has achieved. But off screen, I'm just me – a normal boy, who has friends, goes shopping, goes partying, eats and drinks sometimes a bit too much, but come on, I'm a council estate boy who drank cider on the swings at fifteen! Even if it doesn't make sense to other people, I like watching football and drinking a can of lager as much as I love hitting the shops with my girls. I can't be anything different from what I am.

Sometimes all the fame and celebrity feels as though it's just on loan. That it isn't really mine. And it might all go away one day. If it does, I'll still be proud of how far 've travelled and what I've done. The reality is, I know I could have easily ended up at the bottom of the pile, daydreaming my life away, but I decided a long time ago I wanted more from life than to just get by.

I never set out to be a celebrity. I wanted to be an actor so that I could hide and be anyone else but me. All I ever wanted was to be happy in my skin and with myself, and I think I've almost achieved that. I've accepted that my scared, vulnerable, bullied self will always exist alongside my confident, successful, outgoing self – and I think I'm happy with that. In fact, without both elements, I wouldn't be as good at my job.

People who know about my past always want to know how I became thin. Now you know I did it in one of the worst ways possible. I am not ashamed I starved myself because I have learned to deal with my regrets. But I will never forgive myself for scaring my family.

Am I cured? I'm not sure. In many ways, I am better. I've accepted my complex relationship with food and learned to live with it. But anorexia is insidious. It never goes away and it has come back to visit me several times over the years, when I've felt low, out of control, lacking in confidence and a failure. I've managed to beat it each time but it's always lurking, waiting to pounce on me and pull me back into its grip.

Sometimes, just before I go to sleep, a thought floats into my mind ... *Tomorrow, I'll start my diet* ... and that's the danger signal. That alerts me to be on my guard. The truth is, many battles are over but the war is not yet won. I don't know if it ever will be. But with the strength I have found over the years I am now able to fight it.

The whole area of food and my weight is difficult for me because I am a person who has changed my body and yet I ask women to accept themselves the way they are. I will always struggle with the fact that this is a contradiction. But no matter what my own problems have been, I firmly believe that you've got to embrace who you are as a person. You do not need to lose weight because you look in a magazine and see a woman who is airbrushed, re-touched, underweight and on a catwalk. And I know that because I've been on both sides of the fence. There's no point in losing weight and becoming addicted to the gym if you don't understand the person you are. You can never be happy that way. Accepting who and how you are and resolving to make the most of that person is the key. I truly believe that.

Today, I've found my stride. I know what I'm good at. I've grown in confidence and I'm beginning to be the person I've always wanted to be. I'm pleased with my relationships, and I've never felt that way before. The last ten years have been amazing and I couldn't have done it without the sources of strength in my life. My friends are crucial. While it's true that these days I do get invited to some glitzy affairs and big celebrity bashes, I'm still the guy who likes to hang out with his friends, and I couldn't live without the love and support of my best mates (you know who you are). Evening drinks by the river, chatting for hours and eating dim sum in Soho are some of the things I live for. Thank you.

I am now thirty-five. I have friends for life I will always love, respect, depend on and, more importantly, trust. You are my sight when life has blinded me and you are my touch when I am numb. Thank you for allowing me to be the person I have become.

My other great source of strength is, of course, my agent, Carol. I could go on for chapters about how much I owe her, but she wouldn't like that. Carol has looked after me so well over the last ten years. She's my protector, my personal Rottweiler and my guardian angel. She manages my career, negotiates my deals, keeps the media at bay and is always looking out for me. She is the first person I talk to when I'm panicked about work and she can always reason with me and sort things out. She knows me so well and I trust her completely. I talk to her about everything, we argue all the time, but she always talks me round because I know she truly cares about me and I have such respect for her judgement.

All I want to know is where we are going next on this exciting journey of ours...! *Lilililililililili!*

This brings me to my greatest source of strength – my beloved family. Once, on holiday in Singapore, I missed my family so much that I had four small tattoos, little stick figures to represent each one, done on the inside of my right arm, each expressing a facet of their character. In a strange way it allows me to be forever young.

On the right is Kwok-Lyn, my amazing brother, who shares my sense of humour, accepts me exactly as I am and is my oldest friend. He is my safe place. I know that life has only just begun, but I am not afraid of what it may ask of me because I know Kwok-Lyn will always be there to shield me when I am scared. I'm so proud of what he has achieved, and I adore his family, Lisa and their beautiful daughters – there is space reserved for my nieces Maya and Lola in my family tattoo, ready for when they're older.

Next to him is Oilen, my sister ... well, my love for her is overpowering at times. I care so much about what she thinks. In 2008, *The Times* asked Oilen and me to do a piece called 'Relative Values', and after much discussion we agreed. The journalist asked about growing up on the estate, being mixed race, fat and of course about my being gay. It was strange listening to Oilen speak about me, but also moving. She called me kind and caring, and said how worried she'd been about me when I went through my hardest times. She said: 'He's like a spot of glue – he's the physical link that binds us all together.'

It was like I'd been waiting for those words my whole life. I'm proud of Oilen, her work, her cleverness, her spirit, and proud to be her baby brother. Our bond is unique.

Then there are my parents. Dad on the far left, and Mum on his right. Writing this book has reminded me what we have all been through and how much I owe them. Mum is the most non-judgemental person in the world. She never says you are wrong, her door is always open and she will always listen and advise, but only if you want it: if not, she will simply listen. In my eyes she has the gift of love. She is the centre of my world.

Being able to give something back to my parents has meant so much to me. Dad is nearly seventy now, and he and Mum were still working six days a week in the chippy. At last, I've been able to make a huge difference to their lives – I've been able to pay off their mortgage, so they can finally retire. They are still totally in love and only happy when they are together, and it's now time they celebrate their love without distraction.

What I have – all of it – is down to my parents, to my family and their support. They have been with me through thick and thin. I'm so happy that I can do this for them after everything they've done for me.

Dear Daddy,

I never realised that one day you would be the one person I would find it hardest to tell 'I love you'. It's not because I love you any less than when I relied on you as a child, it's perhaps because I am afraid one day you will not hear me. You and I are one. I think, behave, shout and laugh like you. I know one day I'll have your toothless smile. You have always called me 'Babe' and that name has protected me. When my life is tough and I feel out of control, I know I have somewhere to hide and leave my stress behind me. That place is in your heart. Thank you. I will always vividly remember picking blackberries with you on the rally. It didn't matter we lived on the estate; you managed to find me somewhere safe to play. Daddy, I know it was hard for you to find time for your family because the restaurant needed you as much as we did, but I need you to know it's okay. You did what you had to do to make a life for us; we never wanted for anything, and it was your hard work that did that. I missed you but I understand. I so fondly remember you kicking the ball into the sky so high, it seemed to get lost in the clouds. In my eyes, my dad is the best footballer in the world. I remember going to work with you aged six, dressed in my tuxedo, my hair slicked to one side with handfuls of your Brylcreem. It felt amazing to look like you.

There is something I've never told you. When I was young I would sometimes go into your and Mum's bedroom, close the door and open your jewellery box. I would sit on the stool facing the big round mirror, put on your rings and pretend I was you. I would watch myself in the mirror, hold my hands to my face and imagine myself as you when I grew up. It was the safest place in the world. I know I've not been the perfect son and I know sometimes you've looked at my life and been concerned about my choices but I want to thank you for always allowing me to make my mistakes. It's that support which makes you the best dad in the world. Daddy, you will always be my hero. I love you.

Acknowledgements

Firstly, so many thanks must go to my family ... without you, I wouldn't have a story to tell. Your undying support and guidance has allowed me to have a life I am not only proud of but also one I now wouldn't change. You are my everything; my first thought in the morning and my last thought at night. I could not exist without you and writing this book has reconfirmed just how much you mean to me. I will love you forever and longer, and even longer than that. Thank you.

My friends ... I regard our friendships as our greatest successes. I would not have all I have today without each and every one of you. We have partied for hours, laughed for days, loved for years and I know we will be friends forever. Thank you.

Carol ... what can I say? Who would have thought we would have got this far? You have shown me friendship and support without compromise. Thank God I found you. Maybe it was destiny ... maybe it was fate ... Whatever brought us together, I am grateful it did, Bubala! Thank you.

Sue Murphy and all at Channel 4 ... Thank you for believing in me even when I didn't. Your vision and nurturing have made me the most confident and happy I have ever been. You have given me a home and a place where I can exist in harmony. Thank you.

Ebury ... As you know I was unsure whether I would ever get to this stage. When we first met, I doubted whether I had the courage, skill or story to write this book: thank you for convincing me otherwise. This has been such a wonderful journey of self-discovery that has allowed me to put so many of my demons to rest. Thank you.

Kirsty ... well ... thank you. I could not have done this had you not been involved. I know you have felt my pain and cried my tears and I am so grateful you did. You have not only shaped my paragraphs, corrected my spelling and made sense of my confusion, you have edited your way into my heart forever.

ALL THE PRODUCTION CREWS I HAVE EVER WORKED WITH ... Thank you, for your knowledge, dedication, loyalty and support. Without every single one of you I would not have had the opportunities and experiences that have made my life so rich and full. Thank you.

My viewers ... Your continued support and loyalty have not only kept me going when I thought I couldn't, you have also played a major role in repairing the confidence of a lonely, fat and insecure boy from Leicester. Had you not tuned in and believed in me, then who knows where I would be today?

I love you all so very much.
Kowkhyn/Babe/Gok/Auntie Gok
x